MAKE YOUR OWN
WEB PAGE!

A Guide for Kids

By Ted Pedersen and Francis Moss

Illustrations by Nate Evans

To Daniel Weizmann,
for helping to create the book;
and to all the kids who read it,
for helping to create the Web in the next millennium

Special thanks to Dana Thomson,
Web Developer and Technical Writer

Library of Congress Cataloging-in-Publication Data
Pedersen, Ted.
    Make your own web page! : a guide for kids / by Ted Pedersen & Francis Moss.
        p. cm.
    Summary: Explains how to set up your own web site, including guidelines for basic planning and
design, help on writing HTML and creating hypertext links, and tips on adding graphics. IBM and
MacIntosh compatible instructions.
    1. Web sites—Design—Juvenile literature. [1. Web sites.]
I. Moss, Francis. II. Title.
TK5105.888.P4224 1998   98–30511
005.7 2—DC21   CIP
                                                                    AC

ISBN 0-8431-7459-5
1 3 5 7 9 10 8 6 4 2

CONTENTS

1 ALL ABOUT WEB SITES 1

Introduction 1

Different Kinds of Web Sites 2

Different Ways to Make a Web Site 4

Before You Start 5

What You Need 5

2 CREATING YOUR WEB SITE 7

The Three Basic Steps 7

Imagining Your Web Site 8

Brainstorming 8

Reviewing Other Sites 9

Making Decisions 9

Gathering Pictures and Materials 10

Writing the Text 10

Planning Your Web Site 11

Deciding How Many Pages You Want 11

Sketching Each Web Page 12

Linking Your Pages 13

Building Your Web Site 14
   Basic HTML 14
   A Practice HTML Document 15
   Headings 20
   Text with Line Breaks and Paragraphs 23
   Bold, Italic, and Underlined Text 26
   Changing the Face of Your Text 29
   Changing the Size of Your Text 31
   Changing the Color of Your Text 31
   Centering Headings 34
   Paragraph Alignment 35
   Horizontal Rules 37
   Lists 40
   Using Tables to Format Your Pages 42
   Background Colors 46
   Adding Pictures 48
   Putting Text and Pictures Together 54
   Linking to Other Pages on Your Web Site 60
   Linking to Other Web Sites 66
   Linking to Other Places on the Same Web Page 69
   Linking to Get E-Mail 72
   Link Colors 77
   Presto! A Finished Web Page 79

3 LAUNCHING YOUR WEB SITE 80
  How to Transfer Files to a Web Server 81
  Promoting Your Web Site 83
  Maintaining Your Web Site 86
  Help Is Everywhere 87

Glossary 88
Index 90
About the Authors 92
HTML Quick List . . . . .inside back cover

1

ALL ABOUT WEB SITES

◄ Introduction ►

Today is the day! Elena runs all the way home from school. The reason she is so excited is that she is finally going to put up her very own Web site on the World Wide Web. Elena has designed and built her Web site all on her own, using HTML code, the programming language in which Web pages are written. Now she is ready to post her pages so that people all over the world will be able to visit her site.

Anyone who has cruised the Internet lately knows that the World Wide Web is a huge network made up of millions and millions of Web sites. There are commercial Web sites sponsored by companies to advertise and sell their products. There are educational Web sites sponsored by museums, wildlife organizations, and government agencies—just to name a few. There are sites sponsored by newspapers and magazines where you can get up-to-the-minute news information, twenty-four hours a day.

But these days, lots of ordinary folks, including kids, are creating their own personal Web sites—sites that focus on their own interests, their hobbies, their families, whatever! And you can, too! Believe it or not, this book will teach you how to do exactly what Elena has done—how to design your own Web page, write it out in HTML (or HyperText Markup Language), and post it on the World Wide Web for everyone to see.

Throughout this book, you'll hear us talking about Web pages and Web sites. A Web site is a collection of one or more interconnected Web pages. You might decide to go the simple route and just make one Web page. Or you can create a Web site with a few different pages and link them together so that visitors can move easily from page to page. It's all up to you. Whatever you decide, this book will give you all the information you need to design and make a Web page or Web site that is all your own.

Do you want to see what Elena's home page looks like? Take a look at the back cover of this book. Do you want to learn how Elena created her Web site? Follow along as we go step-by-step through *Make Your Own Web Page!*

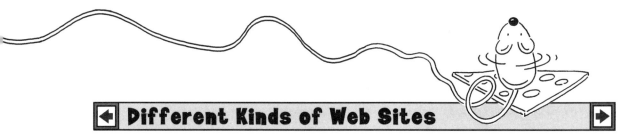

Different Kinds of Web Sites

Today, there are as many different kinds of Web sites on the Internet as there are different kinds of people in the world.

It is a Saturday morning, about a month before Elena posts her site on the Internet. At this point, Elena doesn't know very much about building Web pages. But she knows she likes to surf the Web.

Elena is in her room, at her computer, doing an online search on archaeology for a school project. When she needs to find something on the Internet—and you can find anything on the Internet—Elena always starts at her favorite search site for kids: Yahooligans (**http://www.yahooligans.com**).

As Elena has discovered, it's easy to get distracted from your original Internet search when there are so many other interesting things that you bump into along the way. Soon, Elena gets sidetracked from her archaeology search and finds herself looking for information on her pet gecko. She finds a Web page devoted to pets of all kinds, the **Acme Pet Page** (see below). A little while later, Elena finds a personal Web page that a man has put up, showing pictures of his wife and baby. "Gee, everybody's got a Web page these days," Elena thinks.

Soon, Elena finds herself admiring the images on the **Juggling Information Service** page. Everything you'd want to know about juggling is right there. And before she gets back to her archeology research, she checks out **A Girl's World Online Clubhouse**® to see what's new. After all, she is an official member!

"Most of these pages are pretty nice," Elena thinks to herself. "I wonder how hard it would be to make something like that."

Not hard at all, as we'll see.

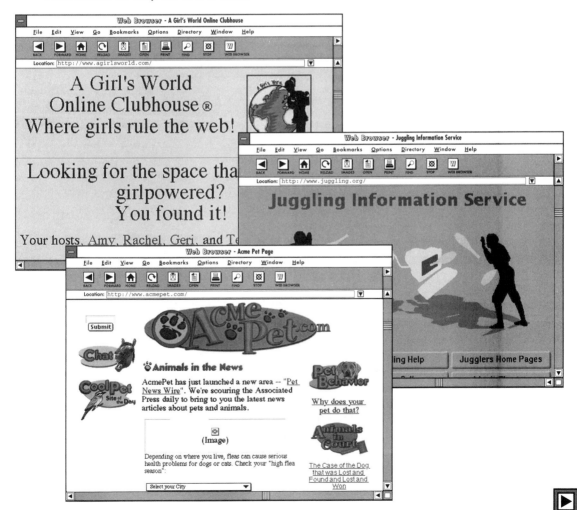

Before you get started, you should know that there are really two ways to create a Web site.

1. You can write it in HTML code, using a program called a *text editor*. Then use a *Web browser* to translate the code and display the Web page as it would appear on the Internet. (We'll talk more about text editors and Web browsers later on in the book.)
2. You can use a special program, like FrontPage, PageMill, or Dreamweaver. With these, you simply tell the program where you want your text and pictures to go on your Web page. Then the programs write the HTML code for you. Prices for these programs start at around $100, and go as high as $500 for those with lots of bells and whistles.

To someone who doesn't know anything about HTML, using a program like FrontPage probably sounds like a great (although expensive) shortcut. You don't necessarily have to learn or understand HTML code to use it. And if that sounds okay to you, then you won't be needing this book!

But we believe that it's a lot smarter to learn HTML and know how to use it to write a simple Web page. Think of it this way: Knowing HTML versus using a program is kind of like knowing how to fish versus getting one free fish dinner. You'll always have food if you know how to fish. And you'll always be able to make a Web page from scratch—any kind of Web page you want to—if you know HTML! You'll speak the language of the Web. And since you'll know all the things that HTML can do, you'll probably end up making cooler, more sophisticated Web pages than you would otherwise.

Plus, HTML is quite easy to learn. But before we go any further, there are a few things you should know before you start planning or designing any Web page.

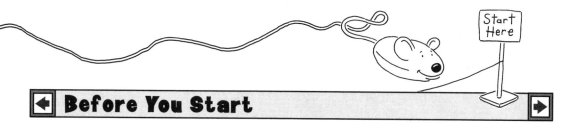

◄ Before You Start ►

Surfing the Internet—and the World Wide Web—is like strolling through a big city. The rules there—stay out of dark places, watch for traffic, don't go with strangers—are the same as on the Net. You probably already know about safe cybersurfing: Don't give out your real name (or at least not your full name), don't give out your telephone number or your address, stay away from restricted Web sites—the usual common sense stuff.

But what is "safe Web design"?

Well, think of your Web site as your house. And think of the visitors to your Web site as guests in your home. You never know who will end up visiting your site, so be courteous and design your site in a way that will make everyone feel comfortable. Don't include material that you know will be offensive to some people. Remember that your site, like your house, will tell the world a lot about you. Make a good impression!

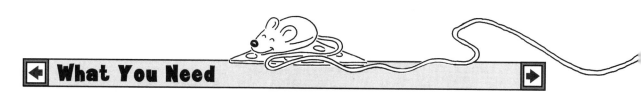

◄ What You Need ►

The quick answer is "Not as much as you think."

You need a computer, of course.

You need a word processing program called a text editor. Simply put, a text editor is a program that allows you to create and edit text files. And since HTML is just a plain-text language, a text editor is all you need to write the HTML code for your Web page. Microsoft Word and WordPerfect are very sophisticated kinds of text editors—but they are actually too sophisticated for what we want to do. It's better to use very simple text editors to write HTML code.

Luckily, if you have Windows on your computer, then you already have an elementary text editor program called Wordpad or Notepad. And if you have a Mac, you have a similar text editor called SimpleText. These are the programs you should use for writing in HTML. (The nice thing about HTML is that you write it the same way, no matter what simple text editor you have.)

You will also need a Web browser program, like Netscape Navigator or Microsoft Internet Explorer. A Web browser reads the HTML code that is written on a text editor. It translates the code and displays it in Web page format. It shows you how your Web page will look on the Internet.

That is everything you need to <u>make</u> your Web page. But in order to post your page on the World Wide Web where people can visit it, you will also need a connection to the Internet. If you already have a modem and Internet access at home, you are all set. If you don't, you can probably use a school or library computer that has Internet access to post your page.

But before we talk about posting a Web page or Web site, we're going to show you, step-by-step, how to make one.

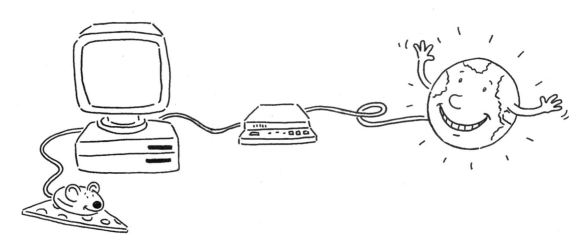

2
CREATING YOUR WEB SITE

◀ The Three Basic Steps ▶

There are three basic steps for getting any Web site ready for the World Wide Web.

1. Imagining Your Web Site

This is the fun part—thinking about and deciding what you want to include on your Web site. The possibilities are endless!

2. Planning Your Web Site

After you decide what you want to include on your Web site, you need to create a simple layout. This is like making a blueprint of the different parts of your Web site and thinking about how they will fit together.

3. Building Your Web Site

At this stage, you type in the actual text of your Web site and insert all of the pictures using HTML, the universal language of the World Wide Web.

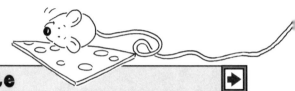

Brainstorming

To begin, brainstorm your ideas. When you brainstorm about something, you write down everything you can think of on the subject. Don't worry if some of the things you think of don't make sense right now. When you come back to them later, they might remind you of something else you want on your list. Or you can cross them off later. But for now, just imagine all the things you might want to include in your Web site.

For example:

❑ You might want to use your Web site to display pictures of your family, friends, or pets.

❑ If you're a budding artist, you can post some of your drawings.

❑ If you have a favorite hobby or interest, you can display information about it on your Web site. There are probably a lot of other kids out there who share your enthusiasm.

❑ If you have a favorite book, you can share it with the rest of the world. If it's a book on a certain time in history, you can display articles and pictures about the time period.

❑ You can use your Web site to create a fan club about your favorite movie star or sports hero.

Whatever you decide, there are two elements that make up most Web sites.

1. **Text.** All the words that appear on your Web site will be written by you! What do you want to say?

2. **Pictures.** These can be family photographs, your school picture, drawings, and so on. Later on in the book, we'll talk about how to get pictures in the right format to use on your Web pages.

Just be careful about copyrights: If a picture is copyrighted, it means that someone else owns it, and you will need that person's permission to use the picture on your Web page. Of course, there's no problem if you want to use your own drawings or photos, so that is often the best way to go. And there are plenty of clip-art packages—which contain neat pictures you can use—available for sale at your local software store or over the Web itself. Copyrights also apply to published text. If you're ever unsure whether it's okay to use something on your Web page, ask a parent or a teacher.

Reviewing Other Sites

As the next step in your Web site building project, take time to do some good old-fashioned browsing around the Web. Pick out a few Web sites—no more than five—that you really like. If you can, print out each page of the Web sites so that you can take a long look at them.

Now, write down three or four elements from each Web site that really appeal to you. What do you like about the way they look? Are they fun to read? Why? Do they have a variety of material on them, or do they focus on one topic? What is it about your favorite sites that makes you want to visit them again and again?

Making Decisions

Eventually, once you've brainstormed and browsed other sites as much as you want to, it's time to make some decisions about your own site. Go back to your original list of ideas and choose the theme (or themes!) of your Web site. You may know that your site is going to be about you. But there are lots of interesting things about you. What do you want to focus on? Think about the specifics.

Need some ideas? How about including one of the following topics?

- ☐ The Coolest Places I've Been
- ☐ The Sports I Love to Play
- ☐ My Friends, and What I Like About Them
- ☐ Smelly Things That Are in My Closet
- ☐ My Best School Subjects
- ☐ My Favorite Foods
- ☐ My Favorite Books, Movies, CDs, and TV Shows
- ☐ The Best Roller Coasters I've Been On

Gathering Pictures and Materials

Finally, if you haven't done it already, you need to get your hands on those visual things you want on your Web site—family photographs, really neat clip art, maybe some of your own drawings. Or perhaps something you wrote in school, like a story or a poem; a favorite recipe; or some notes you have passed in class!

For now, just gather everything you might use and store it in a box.

Writing the Text

At this early stage, you don't have to write the final text for your Web site, but think about what you want to say and start to write it out. Sometimes you won't know what you want to say until you've actually started writing.

Keep your paragraphs short and simple. Remember, most people find it difficult (and boring!) to read a long document on a computer screen. Also, you don't have to do all of your writing in one sitting. Write a little bit, put it aside, and go back to it some other time. Don't be afraid to change what you originally wrote. Even professional writers don't get it right the first time. If you want to, show your text to friends or family members and get their comments. Maybe they will think of some cool things to include that somehow slipped your mind.

Finally, be sure to proofread what you've written for spelling and grammar mistakes.

Planning Your Web Site

Remember when we said that a Web site is like a house? Well, you wouldn't start to build a house without a blueprint, would you? And you shouldn't start building your Web site without a blueprint either. Now that you have a good idea of what you want on your Web site, you need to plan how big you want it to be, how the different pieces will fit together, and how you want it to look when it's all done.

Deciding How Many Pages You Want

When thinking about how many pages you want on your Web site, keep in mind that each of your Web pages should be about a different subject. You need to have enough content on each Web page to fill up a single computer screen.

Take a look at the materials you've gathered. Try to arrange them into piles that represent the different pages you want on your site. If you have several things to say about your favorite hobby, for example, those should all go onto a hobbies page.

Keep your Web site small and simple for now. All Web sites have a *home page*. Like the front page of a newspaper, the home page is the first page you see when you visit a site. Maybe your Web site should have a home page plus two other pages. Three good-looking Web pages are a lot more impressive than a half dozen half-finished pages. And you can always add more pages later. (Rome wasn't built in a day, and neither are Web sites!)

Your three pages might include:
1. A home page, where you introduce yourself, welcome people to your site, and tell them what they can expect to find on your site.
2. A family page, where you can introduce your family—and even your pets.
3. A hobby page, where you tell visitors about your favorite hobbies.

Also, remember that most people surfing the Web have slow connections to the Internet. If your Web site has tons of pictures and a complicated format, it will load onto people's computers very slowly. Some people might get impatient and decide to visit another site instead.

Sketching Each Web Page

Now, for each of your three Web pages, make a pencil sketch of the way you want it to look when it's done. The pages may not turn out exactly the way you sketch them—you might come up with better ideas as we go along—but it's a good place to start.

Take a look at the sketches Elena made for her different Web pages.

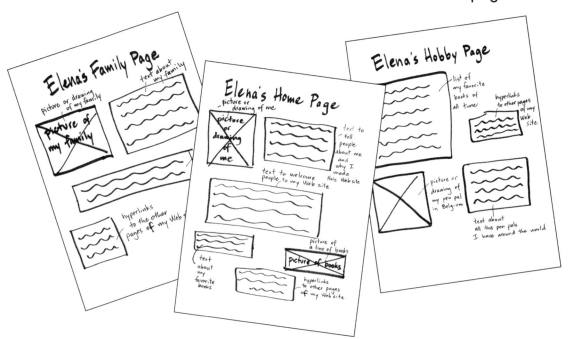

Linking Your Pages

As you probably already know, Web pages are linked to one another by special connections called *hypertext links* (or *hyperlinks*). They are specially formatted words or pictures on a Web page that—when you click on them with your mouse—allow you to jump to a different place on the World Wide Web. They're sort of like electronic passageways. Later on in this book, we'll show you how to add hyperlinks to your own Web site, so that your Web pages are connected to one another. But for now, just think about how you want your pages to be linked.

There are several ways to link your Web site.

You can have each page lead to the next.

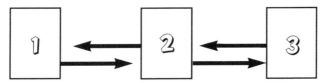

You can link each page to every other page.

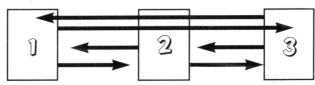

You can link only certain pages.

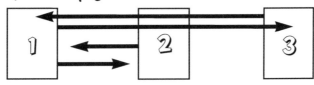

No matter how you decide to link your Web pages, try to keep it simple and always have a link back to the home page on each page of your site.

So, by now you have organized your materials into different Web pages. You have sketched out your Web pages. And you have decided how you would like to link them. Basically you have made all of the preparations you can without actually writing the HTML code that will make it all happen. Now it's time to learn the code.

Basic HTML

As we've said before, all Web pages are written in a language called HTML, which stands for HyperText Markup Language. To create a Web page, you write and edit the HTML code for your Web page in a program called a text editor. Then another program called a Web browser reads the HTML code, translates it into Web-page format, and displays it as a Web page on the computer screen. (Throughout this book, when we talk about a page as seen on a text editor in the form of uninterpreted code, we'll call it an "HTML document." When we talk about a page as it is seen on the Web browser, we'll call it a "Web page.")

When you look at a typical HTML document, it might look like it was written in secret code. But it's not secret. Anyone can write HTML. You only need to know a few rules.

But before we get too bogged down in rules, why don't you open up your text editor and write some actual HTML code? *What?* you say? *I don't know anything about HTML,* you say? Well, for now, you don't have to. Just follow our instructions and type exactly what we tell you to. Together, we'll create a very simple practice Web page. Don't worry if you don't understand what you are typing. You're not supposed to yet! After we've typed in the code, we'll go back and explain it piece-by-piece.

Here we go!

A Practice HTML Document

1. Start by opening your text editor program and creating a new document.

2. On the first line of your document, type in **<HTML>** and press the ENTER (or RETURN) key.

3. Type in **<HEAD>** and press the ENTER key.

4. Type in **<TITLE>** and then type in what you want to call this page. Maybe something like **My Practice Page**. Then type in **</TITLE>** and press ENTER.

5. Type in **</HEAD>** and press ENTER.

6. Type in **<BODY>** and press ENTER.

7. Now type in something like: **Hi. My name is {put in your first name}, and I live in {put in your town}**. Press ENTER.

8. Type **</BODY>** and press ENTER.

9. Now type **</HTML>** and press ENTER to end the document.

10. Finally, SAVE your file on your text editor as a plain text document called **index.html**. If your computer gives you a choice, save it as an ASCII file, or a plain text document. And if your program won't let you use the four-letter extension **.html**, you can shorten it to **.htm**.

Congratulations! You have just created your first complete HTML document. On your screen, you should see something like this:

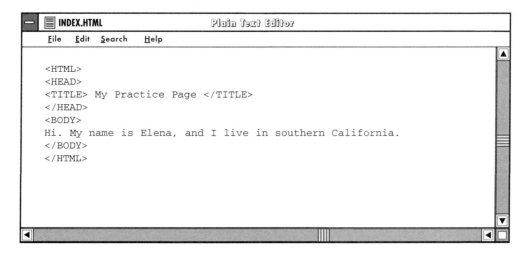

Believe it or not, if you opened up your Web browser and opened this HTML document (**index.html**), you would see a simple Web page on your screen. But we're getting ahead of ourselves. First we are going to explain what it is you just typed.

Take a look at the HTML document on your screen.

You will notice that a lot of the words in the document are between the symbols < and >. These symbols are called *angle brackets*. In HTML, every word or letter that appears between angle brackets is called a *tag*.

Tags tell a Web browser how to read what you have typed in your HTML document, and how to arrange all of that information into a Web page.

Tags often come in pairs. The two tags in a pair look the same, except that the second one begins with a slash symbol (/). For example, look at the first and last tags on the HTML document you typed.

The first tag is <HTML>.

The last tag is </HTML>.

This is a pair of tags. The first one, <HTML>, tells the Web browser that the document that follows will be written in HTML. The tag </HTML> tells the Web browser that it has reached the end of the HTML document. Almost all other pairs of tags work in the same way. The first tag in the pair signals the beginning of something. The second tag in the pair signals the end.

Look at your HTML document again. Right after the <HTML> tag there is another tag: <HEAD>. This tag signals the beginning of a section of your HTML document called the *header*. Everything that comes after <HEAD> but before </HEAD> (two lines below) is part of your header. In our HTML document, the only information contained in the header is the title of our Web page.

On the third line of our document, the <TITLE> tag tells the Web browser that we are about to type in the title of our Web page: "My Practice Page." Then the </TITLE> tag tells the browser it has reached the end of the title. Notice that "My Practice Page" is not between angle brackets. So it is not part of a tag. As we will see later, any text in your HTML document that is <u>not</u> part of a tag will appear on the actual Web page.

On the fourth line, as we mentioned above, we use the </HEAD> tag to mark the end of our header information.

The next tag in our HTML document is <BODY>. This tag signals the beginning of a section of your HTML document called the *body*. Everything that comes after <BODY> and before </BODY> is part of the body. Right now, the only information we have in the body of our document is the line of type containing your name and where you live. Like "My Practice Page," this line of text is not between angle brackets. It is not part of a tag. So this line will also appear on the actual Web page.

As we mentioned above, we signal the end of the body section with the </BODY> tag. Then we signal the end of our HTML document with the </HTML> tag.

Those are all the pieces of your first HTML document. Don't worry if you still don't understand everything about your document. Now we're going to see how it all looks as an actual Web page, and things will become clearer.

To see how your HTML document looks as a Web page, you need to open it in your Web browser program. But don't connect to the Internet, because you don't need to be online. Your Web browser will be looking at documents stored on your own computer's hard drive.

Also, don't close your text editor. As you build your Web page, you will need to keep your text editor and Web browser open at the same time, and switch back and forth between the two.

So, go ahead and open your Web browser. Go to the FILE drop down menu and select OPEN or OPEN A FILE. Type in the directory, folder, and name of your HTML file, as in **c:\myfiles\index.html**. Or look through your directories, using the BROWSE function, until you find your **index.html** file. Open it, and you should see something like this.

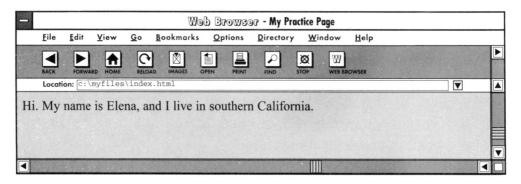

Presto! Your very first Web page!

Let's take a closer look. You'll see that none of the tags from your HTML document appears here. But all the text that was not part of a tag has appeared.

First, the title "My Practice Page" appears in the top bar of your Web browser's window. Remember that in the HTML document, we put the title "My Practice Page" in the header section, between the <TITLE> and </TITLE> tags and within the <HEAD> and </HEAD> tags. Any information that you include in the header section of your HTML document will appear in the top bar of your Web browser. Since we only included the title in our header, that is all that appears.

On the Web page itself, the only text that appears is the line of text you typed between the <BODY> and </BODY> tags in the HTML document. The body of your HTML document is an important section, since it determines what your Web page will actually look like. The body is also usually the biggest section. As we move through the rest of this book, we will spend more time discussing what to put in the body of your HTML document.

In the rest of this section of the book, we will help Elena build her Web page step-by-step. You can follow along, building the same Web page on your computer by doing exactly what we do. If you want to, you can substitute your name for hers, and put in different text and pictures. When we are all done, you will have a Web page that looks something like the one shown on the back cover of this book. You might decide that you want to use this Web page format for your page. Or you can start all over and use what you've learned in this book to build a completely original page.

Let's start with a clean slate; or, in other words, a blank Web page. Instead of starting all over with a completely new HTML document, you can use the practice HTML document you just typed and make a few simple changes. That's the beauty of HTML. You can add or subtract things from your code and then go into your Web browser to see how the changes have affected your Web page.

Click on your text editor window to go back into your **index.html** document.

1. Put your cursor on the third line of your document and delete **My Practice Page**. In its place, type in **Elena's Home Page** between the <TITLE> tag and the </TITLE> tag. (You can substitute your name.)

2. Now put your cursor on the sixth line of your document and delete the entire line of text. Be sure, though, not to delete the <BODY> and </BODY> tags that come before and after.

3. Finally SAVE your file on your text editor as **index.html** (or **index.htm**). Remember to always save it as an ASCII plain text file.

Now your HTML document should look like this.

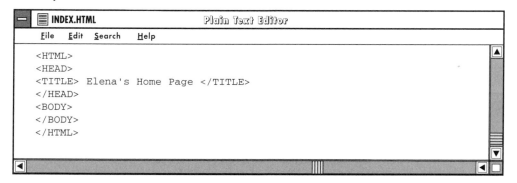

```
INDEX.HTML                    Plain Text Editor
  File   Edit   Search   Help

<HTML>
<HEAD>
<TITLE> Elena's Home Page </TITLE>
</HEAD>
<BODY>
</BODY>
</HTML>
```

To see what your revised HTML document looks like as a Web page, you need to click on your Web browser window to go back into your Web browser program. When you go back into your browser, you might notice that the Web page looks the same as it did before. That's because some Web browsers won't update your Web page automatically. If this is the case for your Web browser, you must locate a command called either REFRESH or RELOAD on your browser menu. Click on it, and your Web page will be updated.

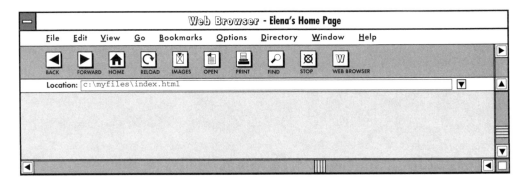

What has changed on your Web page? For one thing, the title in the Web browser window has changed. Where it used to say "My Practice Page," it now reads "Elena's Home Page." That's because you changed the title in the header section of your HTML document.

In addition, now the Web page itself is completely blank. That's because you deleted the one and only line of text that was in the body section of your HTML document.

Now that you've got yourself a blank Web page, let's move on and learn more about what you can put on it.

Headings

Elena has created her first Web page—but when she looks at it in her Web browser, it's completely blank! Now she needs to add some text. First of all, she would like to give her Web page a nice big heading right at the top—sort of like a headline in a newspaper or a title on

the cover of a book. But how can she make larger-than-normal-sized type appear on her page?

Putting headings on different sections of your Web page is a good way to break up your text and let people know what each section is about. You can make headings in lots of different sizes, just by using different heading tags. (Note: Don't confuse "heading" with the "header" section of your HTML document.)

There are six different heading tags: <H1>, <H2>, <H3>, <H4>, <H5>, and <H6>. In each tag, the number indicates the size of the heading as it will appear on the Web page—from <H1>, which is the biggest, to <H6>, which is the smallest.

<H1>	Biggest		<H4>	About normal
<H2>	Very big		<H5>	Smaller
<H3>	Bigger than normal		<H6>	Smallest

These tags are turned off using the corresponding end tags </H1> through </H6>. Any text that you put between a pair of heading tags will appear on your Web page in that type size.

Elena decides to create her heading in the second largest (or <H2>) size. To do so, she follows these steps.

1. Put your cursor after the <BODY> tag and press ENTER to start a new line.

2. Type in **<H2>**. Then type in **Elena's Home Page**. Type **</H2>** to end the heading.

3. SAVE your file.

Now Elena's HTML document looks like this.

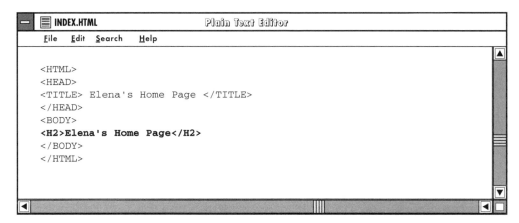

> **Note:** The new line of HTML code we just added is highlighted above in bold-face type. As we continue to build Elena's Web page step-by-step, we'll highlight each new piece in boldface so it is easier to see.

Now when you switch over to the Web browser, the Web page looks like this. (Remember to use your REFRESH or RELOAD command to update your Web page if your Web browser requires it.)

> **Tip:** You can experiment by changing the <H2> tag to a different size heading tag, like <H1> or <H3>, and seeing how it looks on your Web page. But when you do make changes, don't forget to change both of the tags in a pair—the opening tag (or "on" tag) and the end tag (or "off" tag).

Text with Line Breaks and Paragraphs

Elena is very happy with the way her heading turned out. Now she wants to start adding normal-sized type to her page. So she starts typing text into the body of her HTML document. After the </H2> tag, she presses ENTER and types:

Hi! My name is Elena, and this is my Little House on the Web.

I made it…

to tell everyone about me
to link up with my friends
to get extra credit from Mr. Abee
to have the coolest place in cyberspace

Then she saves her revised HTML document and switches over to her Web browser to see how her page looks now. But when the Web page appears on the screen, Elena notices that all of the text she typed in the body is squished together, like this:

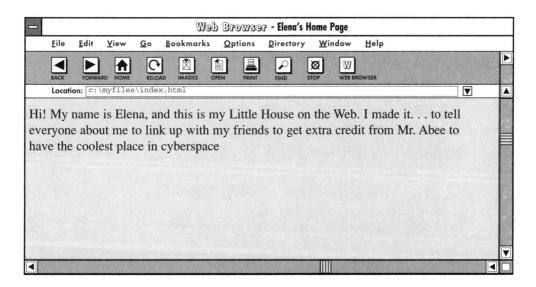

Hey, that's not the way she typed it! What happened to all of the line breaks that Elena typed in using her ENTER key?

Before you start typing a lot of text into your HTML document, you need to know that Web browsers do not recognize line breaks and other formatting that you use with word processors. Remember when we told you that the Web browser ignores all of the ENTERs you type before and after tags in your HTML document? (See tip on page 16.) Well, the same is true for text that you type inside the body of the HTML document—text that you want to appear on your Web page. Instead of using the ENTER key, you need to use the proper tags to tell the browser where to start new lines of text or skip lines. Otherwise, the lines of text on your page will be continuous—with no line breaks—and they will run the whole width of the computer screen.

Use the <BR> tag, or line break tag, to tell the browser to end one line of text and begin a new one. This tag, unlike most tags, does not come in a pair. There is no </BR> tag.

The <P> tag, or paragraph tag, is a shorter way of writing two <BR> tags in a row. The <P> tag tells the browser to end one line of text, skip a line, and begin a new line of text. The <P> tag does have an end tag, </P>, which signals the end of a paragraph. This tag doesn't actually do anything. The Web browser won't notice if you leave it out. But including the </P> at the end of each of your paragraphs is a good idea and it makes your HTML document eaiser to read.

Also, if you type two or more <P> tags in a row, the Web browser will only read the first <P> tag and ignore the ones that come right after. So if you want to skip a few lines on your Web page, use several <BR> tags instead, like this:

.

> **Tip:** When writing your HTML code, place your <P> and <BR> tags at the beginning of the line, where they are easier to see.

Here's how we can write Elena's HTML code so that the text on her Web page comes out the way she wants it.

1. Put your cursor at the end of the </H2> header line, and press ENTER.

2. Type **<P>** to start a new paragraph. Type your welcoming statement: **Hi! My name is Elena, and this is my Little House on the Web.** Type **</P>** to end the paragraph. Press ENTER.

3. Now type **<P>** to start another new paragraph and type **I made it…** Type **</P>**. Press ENTER.

4. Type in **
** to start a new line. Type **to tell everyone about me** and press ENTER.

5. Type **
to link up with my friends** and press ENTER.

6. Type **
to get extra credit from Mr. Abee** and press ENTER.

7. Type **
to have the coolest place in cyberspace** and press ENTER.

8. SAVE the file.

The new HTML document looks like this. (Remember we've put the new lines of code in boldface type.)

```
┌──────────────────────────────────────────────────────────────────┐
│ ─ │ ▤ INDEX.HTML          Plain Text Editor                    │
├──────────────────────────────────────────────────────────────────┤
│   File   Edit   Search   Help                                      │
├──────────────────────────────────────────────────────────────────┤
│    <HTML>                                                          │
│    <HEAD>                                                          │
│    <TITLE> Elena's Home Page </TITLE>                              │
│    </HEAD>                                                         │
│    <BODY>                                                          │
│    <H2>Elena's Home Page</H2>                                      │
│    <P>Hi! My name is Elena, and this is my Little House on the Web.</P> │
│    <P>I made it…</P>                                               │
│    <BR>to tell everyone about me                                   │
│    <BR>to link up with my friends                                  │
│    <BR>to get extra credit from Mr. Abee                           │
│    <BR>to have the coolest place in cyberspace                     │
│    </BODY>                                                         │
│    </HTML>                                                         │
│                                                                    │
└──────────────────────────────────────────────────────────────────┘
```

And here's how the updated Web page looks. Exactly how Elena wanted it.

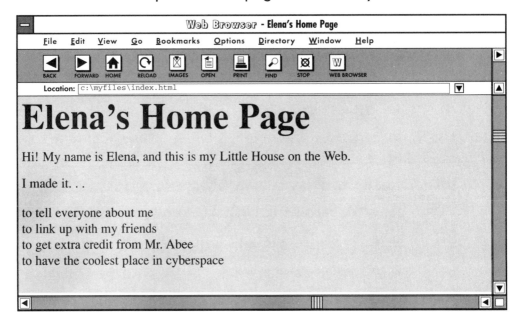

Bold, Italic, and Underlined Text

Before she knows it, Elena is feeling more comfortable about formatting her text using tags. And she is feeling proud of her Web page so far, so she shows it to her mother.

Elena's mother asks her a question: "What if you wanted some words to stand out? Aside from your big heading, all of the text looks the same."

"Easy, Mom," Elena says. "I can make words stand out in a lot of ways."

Okay. You have your text. You've typed it into the body of your HTML document, along with all of the line break tags and paragraph tags you want. But on your Web page, it looks kind of plain. Don't worry! There are plenty of tags you can use to add different typefaces to your text.

Boldfaced text: Everything that you type between the tags <B> and </B> will be boldfaced on your Web page.

Italic text: Everything that you type between the tags <I> and </I> will be italicized on your Web page.

<u>Underlined text</u>: Everything that you type between the tags <U> and </U> will be underlined on your Web page.

Now let's use some of these tags to jazz up Elena's text.

1. Return to **index.html**. Put your cursor after the first <P> tag and before the word "Hi!"

2. Type **<B>** to mark the beginning of the boldfaced text.

3. Put your cursor after "Hi!" and type **</B>** to mark the end of the boldfaced text.

4. Put your cursor just before the words "Little House" and type **<I>** to mark the beginning of the italicized text.

5. Put your cursor between the word "Web" and the period (.) and type **</I>** to mark the end of the italicized text.

6. SAVE your file.

Make sure that the HTML document now looks like this.

```
INDEX.HTML                    Plain Text Editor
File   Edit   Search    Help

<HTML>
<HEAD>
<TITLE> Elena's Home Page </TITLE>
</HEAD>
<BODY>
<H2> Elena's Home Page </H2>
<P><B>Hi!</B> My name is Elena, and this is my <I>Little House on the
Web</I>.</P>
<P>I made it…</P>
<BR>to tell everyone about me
<BR>to link up with my friends
<BR>to get extra credit from Mr. Abee
<BR>to have the coolest place in cyberspace
</BODY>
</HTML>
```

Now when you view the Web page on the browser, Elena's text has been formatted like this.

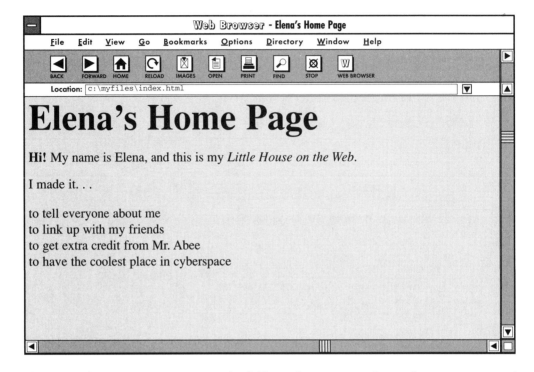

The word "Hi!" appears in boldfaced type, and "Little House on the Web" appears in italicized type.

What if you want to make a word or line of text appear on your Web page in <u>both</u> boldface and italics? That's no problem, either. You just need to use both tags. For example, let's say that Elena wants the word "Hi!" to appear in both boldface and italics.

Instead of **<B>Hi!</B>**, as we wrote the code above...
...we would write it as: **<B><I>Hi!</I></B>**.

Notice that the order of the opening tags (<B><I>) is not the same as the order of the closing tags (</I></B>). The order has been reversed. It is important to remember to close (or turn off) the most recently opened tag first.

Elena's mother nods approvingly as she sees the results on the browser screen. "Very nice, Elena," she says. "But can you do the same thing with different type fonts and colors?"

Elena grins. "No problema, Mama."

Changing the Face of Your Text

In addition to making your text italic, boldfaced, and underlined, you can also specify what *font* you want your text to be in. As you probably already know, fonts are styles of type. There are thousands of different fonts in the world—some very fancy and some very plain—but a computer only has certain fonts installed on it. Among the more common fonts are Times New Roman, Arial, and Helvetica.

If you don't specify a font in your HTML document, the Web browser will just use its standard, or *default* font, and display the text of your Web page in that font. However, if you want to pick a particular font for your page, you can use the <FONT> tag.

The <FONT> tag is a little different from the other tags we have discussed so far. By itself, it doesn't do anything. In order to make it work, you need to add some information inside the <FONT> tag itself.

Here's an example of a line of code using the <FONT> tag. To make this code eaiser to read, we put the tags in boldface type.

<FONT FACE="arial">Hi!**</FONT>**

The first tag in this line of code is <FONT FACE="arial">. It's a longer tag than any of the others we've seen so far. But it's a pretty simple tag. FACE is an *attribute* of the tag. Attributes are additional parts of a tag that give the Web browser more instruction on what to do with the text that follows the tag. When they are added, attributes go right inside the angle brackets of the tag. Not all tags have attributes added to them. But the <FONT> tag is one tag that won't work without an attribute added.

In the example above, <FONT FACE="arial"> tells the Web browser to display the text "Hi!" in the Arial font, or typeface. The end tag </FONT> tells the Web browser to turn the Arial font off.

Here's another example, with the tags in boldface type.

<FONT FACE="helvetica">Hi!</FONT>

This line of code tells the Web browser to display the text "Hi!" in the Helvetica font. The end tag </FONT> tells the Web browser to turn the Helvetica font off. Notice that the font names in the opening tag are placed inside quotation marks.

A Web browser can only display a font that is installed on that computer. So what happens if the Web browser reading your HTML document doesn't have the font you choose? It will simply display the text in its standard default font. But maybe you want to pick a second-choice font for the Web browser to try before it uses its default font. You can do this by writing your code like this.

<FONT FACE="helvetica, arial">Hi!</FONT>

This line of code tells the Web browser to display the word "Hi!" in Helvetica, or in Arial if it doesn't have Helvetica. You can list as many choices of fonts inside the quotation marks as you like. Just separate each font name with a comma and list them in order of your preference: first choice, second choice, third choice, and so on. If the Web browser goes through all of your preferences and doesn't have any of them, then it will display your text in its default font.

> **Tip:** You can also use a general font category —"serif" or "sans serif"— to specify the basic type of font you want. <FONT FACE="serif"> will give you a font like Times New Roman. <FONT FACE="sans serif"> will give you a font like Arial or Helvetica. This is helpful if you don't know the exact name of the font.

Note: Try to choose the most common fonts for the text of your Web page. Then visitors to your Web page will see your page exactly the way you intended it to look.

Changing the Size of Your Text

You can also specify the size of your text using the <FONT> tag. Unlike heading tags, where <H1> was the largest and <H6> was the smallest, font sizes get larger as the numbers go up. Font size 1 is the smallest and font size 7 is the largest. Font size 2 is just about normal-sized type.

Here's an example of how to use the <FONT> tag to specify the size of your text.

<FONT SIZE=4>Hi!</FONT>

SIZE is another attribute of the <FONT> tag. The above tag <FONT SIZE=4> tells the Web browser to display the word "Hi!" in font size 4 type. Then the </FONT> tag tells the browser to turn this font size off.

Changing the Color of Your Text

Finally, you can specify the color of your text using the <FONT> tag. Here's an example.

<FONT COLOR="blue">Hi!</FONT>

COLOR is another attribute of the <FONT> tag. This line of code tells the Web browser to display the word "Hi!" in blue-colored type. Then the </FONT> tag tells the Web browser to turn the blue type off.

In this example, we simply typed the word "blue" in quotation marks to specify the type color we wanted. But not all Web browsers can understand color names. Older Web browsers need to be given a number called a *hex code* in order to understand what color you mean. Let's look at an example of a tag that uses a hex code.

The hex code for the color blue is #0000FF. So we could specify the type color blue using this line of code.

<FONT COLOR="#0000FF">Hi!</FONT>

This tag also tells the Web browser to display the word "Hi!" in blue type. But while some Web browsers won't understand the color word "blue," <u>all</u> Web browsers will understand the hex code for blue. If you want to be sure that your colors come out correctly on all Web browsers, use hex codes instead of color words.

Here is a list of the sixteen color words that most Web browsers can understand, along with the hex codes for each color.

• AQUA	#00FFFF	• BLACK	#000000
• BLUE	#0000FF	• MAGENTA	#FF00FF
• GRAY	#808080	• GREEN	#008000
• LIME	#00FF00	• MAROON	#800000
• NAVY	#000080	• OLIVE	#808000
• PURPLE	#800080	• RED	#FF0000
• SILVER	#C0C0C0	• TEAL	#008080
• WHITE	#FFFFFF	• YELLOW	#FFFF00

Now you know how to use the <FONT> tag to choose a font for text, to choose a size for text, and to choose a color for text. The next thing you will learn is how to do all three of these at the same time.

What if you wanted to tell the Web browser to display the word "Hi!" in the Arial font, in the font size 4, and in the color blue? Believe it or not, you could squeeze all of this information into a single <FONT> tag. This is how you would write it.

<FONT FACE="arial" COLOR="blue" SIZE=4>Hi!</FONT>

That's all there is to it! In this example, there are three attributes (FACE, COLOR, and SIZE) in the <FONT> tag. These attributes can come in any order inside the tag, as long as FONT comes first. You don't even have to separate them with commas. The end tag </FONT> turns off everything in the preceding <FONT> tag.

Why don't we add a nice big <FONT> tag to Elena's HTML document? By now you're getting to be such an expert at making changes to your **index.html** document that we won't even tell you how to add the new code step-by-step. Just input all the changes that we have highlighted in bold-face below, and your new HTML document will look like this.

```
INDEX.HTML                    Plain Text Editor
File   Edit   Search   Help

<HTML>
<HEAD>
<TITLE> Elena's Home Page </TITLE>
</HEAD>
<BODY>
<H2>Elena's Home Page</H2>
<FONT SIZE=2 COLOR="blue" FACE="arial, helvetica">
<P><B>Hi!</B> My name is Elena, and this is my <I>Little House on the
Web</I>.</P>
<P>I made it...</P>
<BR>to tell everyone about me
<BR>to link up with my friends
<BR>to get extra credit from Mr. Abee
<BR>to have the coolest place in cyberspace
</FONT>
</BODY>
</HTML>
```

Don't forget to save the changes to your **index.html** document before you open your Web browser to see the updated Web page. Now, except for the big heading "Elena's Home Page," all the text on the page appears in Arial, font size 2. The text has also turned blue, but since this book is in black-and-white, we can't show you the color transformation here. If you have been following along and making this Web page on your own computer, you will be able to see all of the font and color changes on your screen.

Elena clicks on the REFRESH button on her browser as her mom watches. Suddenly the text turns blue, and the size and font of the text changes.

"You make it look so easy, Elena," her mother says.

"It is easy, Mom," Elena says. "Pretty soon you'll have a Web site of your own." Elena clicks on her text editor window and begins typing. "Now I'm going to put the words in different places on the page," she explains. "Hmm... I wonder how I can make my title heading centered on the page...."

Centering Headings

Elena's text looks nice, but it's all squeezed over against the left margin. How do we change where the text appears on the page?

Well, one way to center headlines is by using the <CENTER> and </CENTER> tags. Here's an example, with the tags shown in boldface.

<CENTER> Elena's Home Page **</CENTER>**

Everything between the <CENTER> and </CENTER> tags will appear centered on the Web page. These tags are exactly what Elena needs to center her title heading. So let's do it.

```
INDEX.HTML                    Plain Text Editor
 File   Edit   Search   Help

<HTML>
<HEAD>
<TITLE> Elena's Home Page </TITLE>
</HEAD>
<BODY>
<CENTER>
<H2>Elena's Home Page</H2>
</CENTER>
<FONT SIZE=2 COLOR="blue" FACE="arial, helvetica">
<P><B>Hi!</B> My name is Elena, and this is my <I>Little House on the
Web</I>.</P>
<P>I made it…</P>
<BR>to tell everyone about me
<BR>to link up with my friends
<BR>to get extra credit from Mr. Abee
<BR>to have the coolest place in cyberspace
</FONT>
</BODY>
</HTML>
```

On the updated Web page the heading is now centered.

```
Web Browser - Elena's Home Page
 File   Edit   View   Go   Bookmarks   Options   Directory   Window   Help

 BACK  FORWARD  HOME  RELOAD  IMAGES  OPEN  PRINT  FIND  STOP  WEB BROWSER

 Location: c:\myfiles\index.html
```

Elena's Home Page

Hi! My name is Elena, and this is my *Little House on the Web*.

I made it. . .

to tell everyone about me
to link up with my friends
to get extra credit from Mr. Abee
to have the coolest place in cyberspace

Paragraph Alignment

You can can choose the alignment of the paragraphs on your Web page by using the paragraph tag, <P>, and putting the ALIGN attribute inside it. (Remember that the <P> tag by itself will end one line of text, skip a line, and begin a new paragraph.)

The <P ALIGN=CENTER> tag will center the text that follows it.

The <P ALIGN=RIGHT> tag will align text against the right side of the Web page.

The <P ALIGN=LEFT> tag will align text against the left side of the Web page. If you use the plain old <P> tag without the ALIGN attribute, the Web browser will automatically left align your paragraph. You should use the </P> end tag to turn these tags off. However, if you don't, the next new paragraph tag will automatically turn them off.

Let's say that you want a paragraph to be left aligned. But you don't want it to appear all the way against the left side of your screen. You can indent your paragraph using the <BLOCKQUOTE> tag. Text that you put between the <BLOCKQUOTE> and the </BLOCKQUOTE> tags will appear on your Web page as though there is a small margin between the text and the left edge of your Web page.

Let's try it out on Elena's page. By adding the new lines of code highlighted below, you will blockquote all of the text that comes after Elena's heading.

```
INDEX.HTML                    Plain Text Editor
File   Edit  Search   Help

<HTML>
<HEAD>
<TITLE> Elena's Home Page </TITLE>
</HEAD>
<BODY>
<CENTER>
<H2>Elena's Home Page</H2>
</CENTER>
<FONT SIZE=2 COLOR="blue" FACE="arial, helvetica">
<BLOCKQUOTE>
<P><B>Hi!</B> My name is Elena, and this is my <I>Little House on the
Web</I>.</P>
<P>I made it…</P>
<BR>to tell everyone about me
<BR>to link up with my friends
<BR>to get extra credit from Mr. Abee
<BR>to have the coolest place in cyberspace
</BLOCKQUOTE>
</FONT>
</BODY>
</HTML>
```

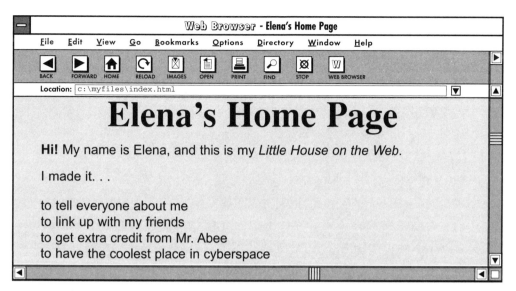

See the difference? The text is still neatly lined up, but now it is pushed over slightly to the right, so that it is not right up against the left side of the page.

You can also "nest" blockquotes. If you put a <BLOCKQUOTE> tag within text that is already blockquoted, you will end up with indented text within indented text on your Web page.

> **Tip:** Heading tags (<H1> through <H6>) and <BLOCKQUOTE> tags automatically insert appropriate spacing before and after the text you put inside them. You can add <P> or <BR> tags to give you more spacing if you prefer. But if you don't, these tags will make sure that your headings and your blockquoted paragraphs don't get squished into other text that comes before or after.

Horizontal Rules

One cool way to divide the sections of your Web page is by using the <HR> tag to make *horizontal rules*. A horizontal rule is a line drawn across your page, like this:

You can put a horizontal rule anywhere on your Web page. You can also put a line break tag (<BR>) before and after the <HR> tag to add more space above and below the rule. Like the line break tag <BR>, the <HR> tag is a stand-alone tag. It does not come in a pair.

Tip: You can use horizontal rules to separate blocks of text on your Web page, like headings and main text. Horizontal rules are simple and powerful tools in Web page design, but be careful not to overuse them.

If you insert the <HR> tag into your HTML document, the rule on your Web page will run the entire width of your page. But suppose you don't want it to be that wide. You can specify the width of a horizontal rule by using the WIDTH attribute inside the <HR> tag. For example:

<HR WIDTH=500>

This tag will make a horizontal rule on your page that is 500 *pixels* wide. Pixels are a unit of measurement on a computer screen. Most screens are at least 600 pixels wide. You can experiment with the width of your rule by changing the number of pixels. The larger the number, the longer the rule. The smaller the number, the shorter the rule.

You can also use the ALIGN attribute inside the <HR> tag to specify the alignment of the horizontal rule.

<HR ALIGN=CENTER> will make a rule that is centered on your Web page.

<HR ALIGN=LEFT> will make a rule that is left aligned on your Web page.

<HR ALIGN=RIGHT> will make a rule that is right aligned on your Web page.

If you don't use the ALIGN attribute, the Web browser will automatically center your horizontal rule.

You can control the thickness of your horizontal rule by using the SIZE attribute inside the <HR> tag. Ordinarily, the <HR> tag will make a rule that is about 2 pixels thick. If you want a thinner or thicker rule on your Web page, all you have to do is change the SIZE attribute in the <HR> tag.

<HR SIZE=1> will make a rule that is 1 pixel thick.
<HR SIZE=5> will make a rule that is 5 pixels thick.

Experiment with different sizes of rules until you get the exact thickness you want.

One more thing about horizontal rules. The line that the <HR> tag makes on your page will have a slight shadow behind it. If you don't want a shadow on your rule, simply put the NOSHADE attribute inside the <HR> tag. This will give you a plain solid line.

Just like the <FONT> tag, you can put more than one attribute in an <HR> tag. And you can put them in any order you want. Let's insert a rule on Elena's Web page between her main heading and text. All it takes is one new line of code.

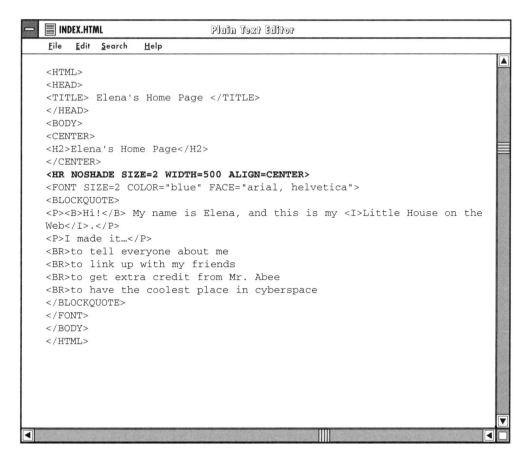

```
<HTML>
<HEAD>
<TITLE> Elena's Home Page </TITLE>
</HEAD>
<BODY>
<CENTER>
<H2>Elena's Home Page</H2>
</CENTER>
<HR NOSHADE SIZE=2 WIDTH=500 ALIGN=CENTER>
<FONT SIZE=2 COLOR="blue" FACE="arial, helvetica">
<BLOCKQUOTE>
<P><B>Hi!</B> My name is Elena, and this is my <I>Little House on the
Web</I>.</P>
<P>I made it...</P>
<BR>to tell everyone about me
<BR>to link up with my friends
<BR>to get extra credit from Mr. Abee
<BR>to have the coolest place in cyberspace
</BLOCKQUOTE>
</FONT>
</BODY>
</HTML>
```

As you can see by looking at Elena's updated Web page in the browser, the new line of code made a thin, unshaded, centered rule that is 500 pixels wide.

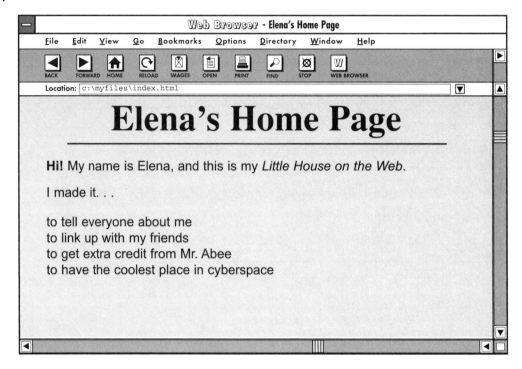

Lists

You probably make and use lists all the time at home and in school. Lists are also really good for organizing information on your Web page. There are two basic types of lists you can make.

Ordered lists, or numbered lists, are the kind you are probably most familiar with. Each item on an ordered list has a number in front of it. You can start an ordered list in your HTML document by using the <OL> tag. Then just put a list tag (<LI>) in front of each item you want on your list. Note that like the <BR> tag, you don't need an end tag (like </LI>) to mark the end of a list item. The <LI> tag automatically shuts off when you put in the next <LI> tag, or when you end the list. To end the list, you must use the </OL> tag.

So, to make an ordered list with three items, you would:

1. Type **<OL>** to start the list and press ENTER.

2. Type **<LI>** and type in the first item you want on the list. Then press ENTER.

3. Type **<LI>** and type in the second item. Then press ENTER.

4. Type **<LI>** and type in the third item. Then press ENTER.

5. Type in **</OL>** to end the ordered list.

Unordered lists use bullets, or small dots, to mark each item in a list. To make an unordered list, you would do the same as you would to make an ordered list. But instead of the <OL> and </OL> tags, you would use the <UL> and </UL> tags to mark the beginning and end of the list.

On Elena's Web page, let's organize some text into an unordered list.

```
INDEX.HTML                    Plain Text Editor

File   Edit   Search   Help

<HTML>
<HEAD>
<TITLE> Elena's Home Page </TITLE>
</HEAD>
<BODY>
<CENTER>
<H2>Elena's Home Page</H2>
</CENTER>
<HR NOSHADE SIZE=2 WIDTH=500 ALIGN=CENTER>
<FONT SIZE=2 COLOR="blue" FACE="arial, helvetica">
<BLOCKQUOTE>
<P><B>Hi!</B> My name is Elena, and this is my <I>Little House on the
Web</I>.</P>
<P>I made it…</P>
<UL>
<LI>to tell everyone about me
<LI>to link up with my friends
<LI>to get extra credit from Mr. Abee
<LI>to have the coolest place in cyberspace
</UL>
</BLOCKQUOTE>
</FONT>
</BODY>
</HTML>
```

We added the <UL> and </UL> tags to mark the beginning and end of our unordered list. And in place of the <BR> tags that we used to have before each line of text, we substituted <LI> tags. When you look at the updated Web page, you will see that the <LI> tags automatically take care of indenting and aligning the items in the list, and inserting line breaks.

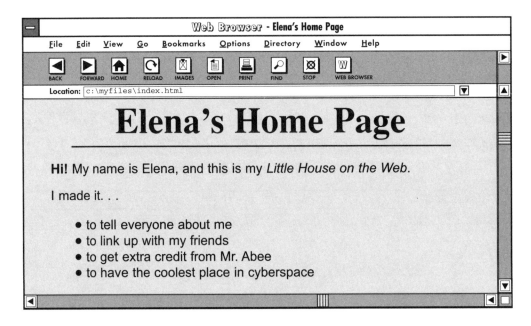

Using Tables to Format Your Pages

After dinner the following day—and after doing her homework!—Elena goes back to her HTML document. She likes the way her Web page is starting to look. But she is confused about one thing. When she makes her Web browser window larger or smaller, some of the formatting on her Web page changes. It still looks okay, but it isn't quite the way Elena had intended it to look. What can she do about that?

A Web browser displays all different sizes of Web pages. And, in most cases, the browser will expand or shrink a Web page to fit the size of the computer screen that is being used. When this happens, the Web page will not look the way it was designed to look.

See for yourself. With your Web browser open, look at our latest version of Elena's Web page. Now, using your mouse, click and drag on one of the top corners of the Web browser window to change its size. Watch what happens to the words on Elena's page as you make the window smaller, and then larger again. See how the text moves around to fit the size of the window?

Luckily, there is a way to make sure that everyone who visits your Web page, no matter what size computer screen or Web browser window they have, will see the page just as you designed it to look. To do this, you can use the table tag, <TABLE>.

The <TABLE> tag has tons of different uses in Web page design. Say you want to put a table on your Web page to keep track of your favorite baseball players' batting averages this season. Or to show people how much your two new puppies have grown in the last few months. You can use the <TABLE> tag to build a neat table with rows and columns.

Here are the basic tags that build a table.

❑ <TABLE> begins a table.

❑ <TR> starts a new *row* across your table.

❑ <TD> starts a new *data cell* within a row. A cell is like a box. It grows as wide as necessary to contain all the information you put in it. </TD> ends a cell.

❑ When you have strung together all of the cells you want in one row, you use </TR> to end a row. Then you can start another row with another <TR> tag.

❑ When you come to the end of the last row in your table, you can end the row with the </TR> tag. Then end the table with the </TABLE> tag.

Using just these few tags, you can build a very simple table or a very complex table. You can even specify how big you want the entire table to be on the screen by using the WIDTH attribute inside the <TABLE> tag. For example, let's say you want your table to be 300 pixels wide. You write it like this.

<TABLE WIDTH=300>

This tag will make sure that the table is always 300 pixels wide, no matter what size the computer screen is. This WIDTH attribute is what makes the <TABLE> tag so useful for formatting your Web page. Why? Because if you put everything in the body of your HTML document (in other words, everything on your Web page) inside a <TABLE> tag and define the width, your Web page will always be that width on every computer screen.

Here. We'll show you. Add these highlighted lines of code to your HTML document.

```
INDEX.HTML                    Plain Text Editor
File   Edit  Search   Help

<HTML>
<HEAD>
<TITLE> Elena's Home Page </TITLE>
</HEAD>
<BODY>
<TABLE WIDTH=600 BORDER=2>
<TR><TD>
<CENTER>
<H2>Elena's Home Page</H2>
</CENTER>
<HR NOSHADE SIZE=2 WIDTH=500 ALIGN=CENTER>
<FONT SIZE=2 COLOR="blue" FACE="arial, helvetica">
<BLOCKQUOTE>
<P><B>Hi!</B> My name is Elena, and this is my <I>Little House on the
Web</I>.</P>
<P>I made it…</P>
<UL>
<LI>to tell everyone about me
<LI>to link up with my friends
<LI>to get extra credit from Mr. Abee
<LI>to have the coolest place in cyberspace
</UL>
</BLOCKQUOTE>
</FONT>
</TD></TR>
</TABLE>
</BODY>
</HTML>
```

Now everything in the body of the HTML document is inside a <TABLE> tag. Everything in the body is also inside a <TR> tag and a <TD> tag, which means that the entire table has only one big row and one big cell. Now your Web page will be 600 pixels wide on every computer screen. You can change this number, but keep it to about 600 pixels or less, which is as wide as many computer screens can view.

You'll also notice that we added another attribute inside the <TABLE> tag. BORDER=2 will put a border about 2 pixels thick around the table—or, in this case, your entire Web page. (If you want a thicker border, just substitute a larger number.)

Save your document and switch to your Web browser to see how the updated page looks.

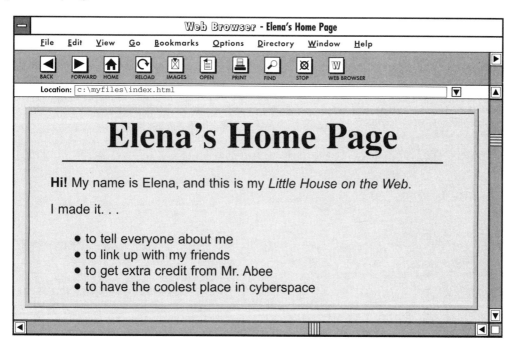

Try playing with the size of your Web browser window now. Do you see how the layout of the Web page stays exactly the same, no matter what the size of the window? Now when the window gets smaller, part of the Web page gets cut off. This is the reason why you should keep the width of your table at 600 pixels or less. If you make the width too much more than 600 pixels, people with small computer screens might not be able to see enough of your Web page.

Take a look at the border around Elena's Web page. We added the border so that you could see exactly what size her new page turns out to be using this <TABLE> tag. But Elena would rather not have the border showing. We can take it away by changing the BORDER attribute to 0.

Why don't you go back and do that? Substitute 0 for the 2 in the BORDER attribute. Then save your document and look at it in the Web browser. If you experiment again with the size of the browser window, you'll see that the Web page behaves the same way with or without the border showing. Even though you can't see the border, the table is still there, keeping the width of the Web page at 600 pixels.

Background Colors

Feel like having more fun with colors? Good! Because text isn't the only thing you can color on your Web page. You can decide what color to make the background, too.

All you need to do is put the background color attribute, or BGCOLOR, inside the <BODY> tag. Here's an example.

```
<BODY BGCOLOR="yellow">
```

This tag, as you probably guessed, will put a yellow background on your Web page.

Notice that the color word "yellow" is inside quotation marks, just as it is when you specify a color for your text inside the <FONT> tag. You can use the same color words and hex codes for background colors as you would use for text colors. (See the list on page 32.)

When you add a tag to specify a background color, the updated HTML document should look like this.

```
<HTML>
<HEAD>
<TITLE> Elena's Home Page </TITLE>
</HEAD>
<BODY BGCOLOR="yellow">
<TABLE WIDTH=600 BORDER=0>
<TR><TD>
<CENTER>
<H2>Elena's Home Page</H2>
</CENTER>
<HR NOSHADE SIZE=2 WIDTH=500 ALIGN=CENTER>
<FONT SIZE=2 COLOR="blue" FACE="arial, helvetica">
<BLOCKQUOTE>
<P><B>Hi!</B> My name is Elena, and this is my <I>Little House on the
Web</I>.</P>
<P>I made it...</P>
<UL>
<LI>to tell everyone about me
<LI>to link up with my friends
<LI>to get extra credit from Mr. Abee
<LI>to have the coolest place in cyberspace
</UL>
</BLOCKQUOTE>
</FONT>
</TD></TR>
</TABLE>
</BODY>
</HTML>
```

When you look at the new Web page in your browser, you will notice that it's a lot more colorful than it was before. We won't show you the updated page here, because we can't illustrate the colored background in our black-and-white book. But you should see a vivid color change on your computer screen.

Experiment as much as you want to with different background and text colors on your Web page. Just keep in mind that some combinations of colored text and colored background (like red text over a bright blue background) might make your page hard to read.

Adding Pictures

Elena is standing at the front door to her house, waiting for her father to come home. Yesterday, Elena gave him the photographs and drawings she wanted to put on her Web site, and her dad had them scanned at an office supply store. Tonight he is bringing them home, and Elena is impatient to add them to her Web pages.

Finally, her father's car pulls into the driveway. Elena's dad gets out of the car, smiling as Elena hurries out to meet him. "What a nice welcome!" he says. Then he pauses, in mock-dismay. "Or are you only after these scanned photos?" He holds up a floppy disk.

Elena kisses her father on the cheek then grabs the disk. "Thanks, Dad," she says as she turns and runs upstairs to her room. Her computer is on; her text editor and Web browser are ready to go. Today Elena is going to add pictures to her page!

Web pages do not live by words alone. You can insert pictures into your page to make it really stand out. But how do you do it? Before you can add any picture to your Web page, you need to make sure it's in the proper format.

There are two basic image formats that Web browsers can understand.

1. The GIF format (you pronounce it "giff" or "jiff") was created by CompuServe and has become a standard for displaying pictures online. It works best for drawings. You can tell that a picture is stored in this format if its file name ends in **.gif**.
2. The JPEG format (you pronounce it "jay peg") is usually used for photographs. You can tell that a picture is stored in this format if its file name ends in **.jpg**.

But what do you do if you want to use a photo or drawing that isn't in one of these formats? There are many programs available that can help you convert your picture to a GIF or JPEG file. Some of them are even available on the Web.

Or what if your picture isn't even a file on your computer yet? What if it's an actual photo or piece of paper that you are holding in your hand? In that case, you can do what Elena's dad did for her. Take the picture to your local printing or graphics store. For a fee, they will scan the image and put it on a floppy disk in GIF or JPEG format. (Just be sure to tell them that you want to use it on a Web page.) Then you can copy the file onto your computer. Save it in the same folder as your **index.html** document.

Finally, don't forget those clip art packages you can buy at office and computer supply stores. Just be sure that the art you buy is in an appropriate format.

Once you have a picture that's in a compatible format, you can add the image to a Web page using the image tag, <IMG>. All by itself, this tag doesn't do anything. You need to use the source attribute, SRC, to identify the file name of the picture you want to add to your Web page.

Here's an example:

```
<IMG SRC="mycats.gif">
```

This tag tells the browser to find an image file called **mycats.gif** and insert it into your Web page. (Notice that you need to put the file name in quotation marks.) Unless you include the name of a directory or folder along with the file name, the Web browser will look for the image file in the same directory as your **index.html** document. So be sure that all of the images you want to use on your site are saved in the same directory as **index.html**.

Images can be placed almost anywhere in your HTML documents. They can be between paragraphs, inside of paragraphs, inside list items, inside tables, or even inserted as part of a heading.

Elena has a drawing that she wants to put on her Web page. It's a drawing that she made of herself sitting in front of her computer. It's already in GIF format—thanks to her dad—and it's called "elenacomputer.gif". So Elena is all set and ready to add her first picture to her Web page. But how big will the drawing be on her page? She doesn't want it to be so big that it overpowers the whole page. And not so small that it can't be seen.

It's very easy to control the sizes of images on your Web page. You just use the WIDTH and HEIGHT attributes inside the <IMG> tag. The WIDTH attribute tells the Web browser how large to make your image from side to side. The HEIGHT attribute tells the browser how large to make it from top to bottom.

Before you decide what size you want your image to be on the Web page, you should find out how large, in pixels, the image is now. How do you do that? You can use a paint program, like Paint Shop Pro (for Windows) or ShareDraw (for Macintosh) to measure the width and height of your image in pixels. If you don't already have a paint program, there are several simple ones that you can get over the Internet.

> **Tip:** Even if you don't want to resize an image, using the WIDTH and HEIGHT attributes (to specify the exact pixel size of the picture) will "reserve" that amount of space on your Web page, making it load cleaner—and often faster—on the viewer's Web browser.

Using her paint program, Elena measures her image and finds out that it is 340 pixels wide and 350 pixels high. Elena decides she would like it to be about half the original size on her Web page. So she divides the width in half to get 170, and divides the height in half to get 175. (Whenever you change the width of an image, you must also change the height of the image in the exact same way. Otherwise, the resized image that appears on your Web page will be out of proportion.)

Now let's add Elena's image to her Web page. Since we will only add one new line of code, we will only show the first half of the revised HTML document—the part that contains the change.

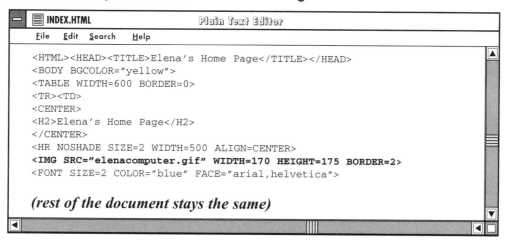

```
INDEX.HTML                          Plain Text Editor
  File   Edit   Search   Help

<HTML><HEAD><TITLE>Elena's Home Page</TITLE></HEAD>
<BODY BGCOLOR="yellow">
<TABLE WIDTH=600 BORDER=0>
<TR><TD>
<CENTER>
<H2>Elena's Home Page</H2>
</CENTER>
<HR NOSHADE SIZE=2 WIDTH=500 ALIGN=CENTER>
<IMG SRC="elenacomputer.gif" WIDTH=170 HEIGHT=175 BORDER=2>
<FONT SIZE=2 COLOR="blue" FACE="arial,helvetica">

(rest of the document stays the same)
```

(Notice that in the above document, we have moved more tags up to the first line. Remember that the Web browser doesn't care whether tags are right next to each other or on separate lines.)

Elena's revised Web page looks like this.

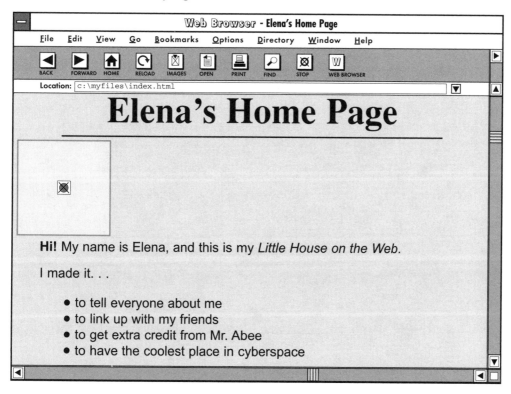

When you look at the revised Web page on your computer, you won't see the drawing that Elena just added. That's because you don't have the file **elenacomputer.gif** on your computer. But you will see a border outlining the space where the image would be. We included the attribute BORDER=2 in our image tag so that you could see exactly where Elena's image would appear on her page. (If you want to see what the new image looks like, take a look at the back cover of this book. It's the black and white drawing on her page.)

You can also include the ALT attribute in an <IMG> tag. ALT stands for alternative text. You can use the ALT attribute to display text in place of an image on your page. Why would you want to do that? Well, in most cases, visitors to your Web site will see the text of your page appear on their screens almost immediately. But they might have to wait longer for the pictures to load. So while people are waiting, alternative text lets them know what kind of picture is on its way. Also, some people turn off the image display on their Web browsers. The Web browser works faster because it doesn't have to load any images at all. But these visitors won't see any of the pictures you put on your page. If you include alternative text for your images, you will let them know what kinds of pictures they're missing.

Here is an example of an <IMG> tag with the ALT attribute.

<IMG SRC="cricket.jpg" ALT="My cat, Cricket">

In this example, **cricket.jpg** is the image file name of a photo of a cat named Cricket. This tag tells the Web browser to insert **cricket.jpg** and to display the alternative text "My cat, Cricket" while the image is loading, or in place of the image if the viewer's image display is turned off. Try to keep ALT text short and to the point, like <ALT="This is me!"> to identify a picture of yourself.

Elena is going to add an ALT attribute to her <IMG> tag. She has also decided that she doesn't want a border around her image, so she will change the BORDER attribute in the <IMG> tag to 0. (You can leave it as BORDER=2 if you still want to keep track of where Elena's image appears on the page.)

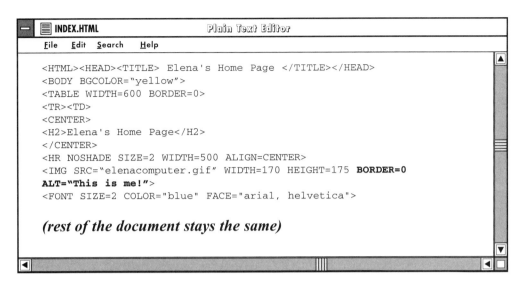

```
INDEX.HTML                    Plain Text Editor
File    Edit   Search    Help

<HTML><HEAD><TITLE> Elena's Home Page </TITLE></HEAD>
<BODY BGCOLOR="yellow">
<TABLE WIDTH=600 BORDER=0>
<TR><TD>
<CENTER>
<H2>Elena's Home Page</H2>
</CENTER>
<HR NOSHADE SIZE=2 WIDTH=500 ALIGN=CENTER>
<IMG SRC="elenacomputer.gif" WIDTH=170 HEIGHT=175 BORDER=0
ALT="This is me!">
<FONT SIZE=2 COLOR="blue" FACE="arial, helvetica">
```

(rest of the document stays the same)

Now when you view the Web page, you will see the text "This is me!" appear in place of Elena's image.

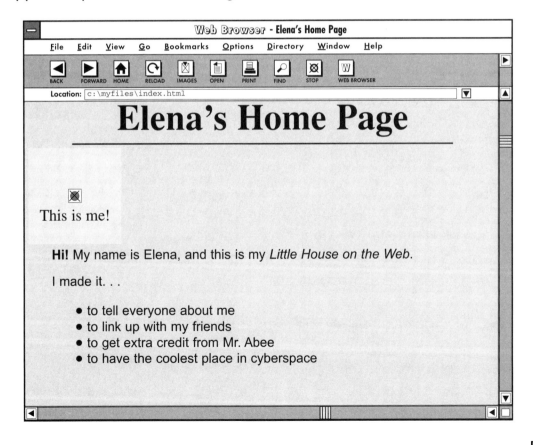

Tip: When you're working on your own computer, text and images on your Web page will load very quickly. But when someone comes to your Web site on the Internet, things will usually be a lot slower. Even if they have a fast modem connection, the Internet (like highways) will be clogged with traffic at certain times of day and downloading will slow to a crawl. Keeping your pages simple and using small graphic files will help visitors load your pages faster.

Putting Text and Pictures Together

Elena looks at the latest version of her home page. She has an image and some text. Her picture comes first on her page (right after her heading), and the text that follows appears underneath the picture. Now Elena wants to make her text appear next to her picture. How can she do that?

To make your Web pages really sparkle, it's important to put images and text together in attractive ways. Wrapping text around an image is one way to do this. Text wrapping makes it possible for an image to be embedded in text (surrounded on three sides). You see examples of text wrapping in books, magazines, and newspapers all the time.

We can use text wrapping to make Elena's picture and her text appear side by side on her Web page. She has two options. She can have her picture appear on the left side of the Web page, with the text to the right of the picture. Or she can have her picture appear on the right side of the Web page, with the text to the left of the picture.

To wrap text around an image, you need to add an ALIGN attribute to your <IMG> tag. Here's an example.

```
<IMG SRC="elenacomputer.gif" ALIGN=RIGHT>
```

The ALIGN attribute in this tag tells the Web browser to place Elena's image (**elenacomputer.gif**) on the right side of her Web page. Any text that comes after this tag in her HTML document will wrap around the left side of the image.

What if Elena wants the image on the left and the text on the right? That's easy. She just changes the ALIGN attribute so that the browser puts the image on the left.

```
<IMG SRC="elenacomputer.gif" ALIGN=LEFT>
```

Now Elena's picture will appear on the left side of the page and any text that comes after the tag will wrap around the right side of the image. So you just use the ALIGN attribute to tell the browser where to put your image, and the text that follows the tag will automatically wrap around the other side.

You can stop (or "turn off") text wrapping around an image by inserting a <BR CLEAR> tag. This stand-alone tag tells the Web browser to wait until the margins of the Web page are clear of images before displaying any more text.

<BR CLEAR=LEFT> tells the Web browser not to display any more text until after the left margin of the Web page is clear of images.

<BR CLEAR=RIGHT> tells the Web browser not to display any more text until the right margin of the Web page is clear of images.

<BR CLEAR=ALL> (or just <BR CLEAR>) tells the Web browser not to display any text until after both margins are clear of images.

So...let's say Elena wants her drawing on the left side of her page and her text next to it on the right. She also wants to add some more text to her page. But she doesn't want the additional text to wrap around her drawing. She wants it to appear below the picture.

Let's add these highlighted lines of code to make it happen. This is a lot of new code to add. But except for the ALIGN attribute and the <BR CLEAR> tag, it's nothing that we haven't done before. And since nothing before the <IMG> tag will change, we will only show you the revised HTML document from the <IMG> on.

(no changes to the document up to this point)

```
<IMG SRC="elenacomputer.gif" WIDTH=170 HEIGHT=175 BORDER=0
ALT="This is me!" ALIGN=LEFT>
<FONT SIZE=2 COLOR="blue" FACE="arial, helvetica">
<BLOCKQUOTE>
<P><B>Hi!</B> My name is Elena, and this is my <I>Little House on
the Web</I>.</P>
<P>I made it…</P>
<UL>
<LI>to tell everyone about me
<LI>to link up with my friends
<LI>to get extra credit from Mr. Abee
<LI>to have the coolest place in cyberspace
</UL>
</BLOCKQUOTE>
</FONT>
<BR CLEAR>
<FONT SIZE=3 COLOR="red" FACE="arial, helvetica">
<BLOCKQUOTE>
Welcome! My Web site is like my room: kind of messy,
but full of lots of real neat stuff!
Follow the links at the bottom of the page to check it out!
</BLOCKQUOTE>
</FONT>
</TD></TR>
</TABLE>
</BODY>
</HTML>
```

Here's what we did. We added the ALIGN=LEFT attribute to the long <IMG> tag. We added the <BR CLEAR> tag to stop the text wrapping after the blue text that Elena already had on her page. Then we added a new batch of text—complete with a new <FONT> tag and SIZE, COLOR, and FACE attributes. And we blockquoted the new text so that it would be indented on the page.

Take a look at the updated Web page on your browser. In this next graphic, we have added Elena's drawing, **elenacomputer.gif**. But remember, since you do not have this image file on your computer, the drawing will not appear on your version of the Web page.

Here is how Elena's Web page looks now.

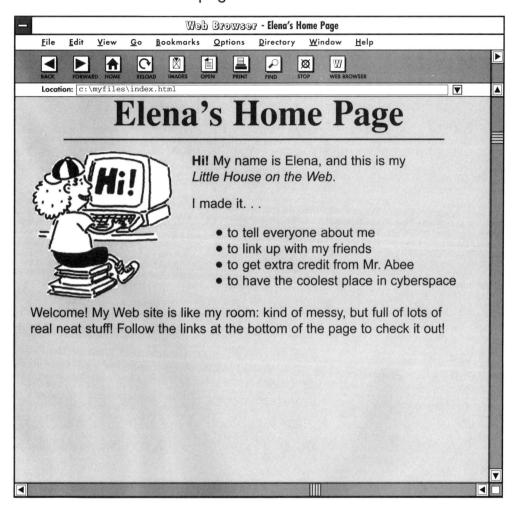

Do you see how the <BR CLEAR> tag stopped the text wrapping after the blue text, so that the red text appears up against the left margin under the image?

"Hey!" Elena thinks. "This is really starting to look like a real Web site. Now, what do I want to do next?" Elena studies her Web page for a while. "Well," she thinks, "the new red text is kind of close to the bottom of my picture. I wonder if there's any way to keep text a certain distance away from the images on my page."

Elena is in luck, because there are two more attributes you can add to an <IMG> tag that will take care of this problem. We can use them to tell the Web browser to keep text a certain distance away from the top, bottom, and sides of an image.

Most browsers will automatically put 2 pixels of space between images and text. That is not very much space at all. You can use the VSPACE and HSPACE attributes to increase the amount of space between the image and the text. Here's an example of an <IMG> tag with VSPACE and HSPACE attributes.

<IMG SRC="elenacomputer.gif" VSPACE=10 HSPACE=15>

This tag tells the Web browser to put 10 pixels of VSPACE (or "vertical space") between the top of the image and any text, and between the bottom of the image and any text. It also puts 15 pixels of HSPACE (or "horizontal space") between the sides of Elena's picture and any text that wraps around it.

Now we are going to add some VSPACE and HSPACE around the picture on Elena's Web page. And we are also going to take out the <BLOCK-QUOTE> and </BLOCKQUOTE> tags around the blue text. Because, as you will see, the HSPACE attribute will take care of formatting our blue text correctly.

Make sure your new HTML document looks like this.

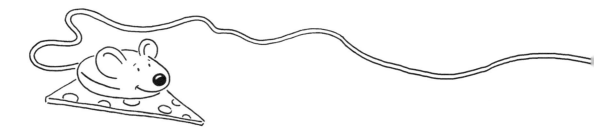

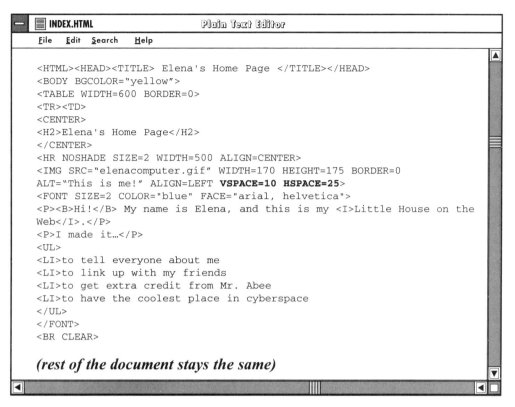

```
INDEX.HTML                    Plain Text Editor

File   Edit   Search   Help

<HTML><HEAD><TITLE> Elena's Home Page </TITLE></HEAD>
<BODY BGCOLOR="yellow">
<TABLE WIDTH=600 BORDER=0>
<TR><TD>
<CENTER>
<H2>Elena's Home Page</H2>
</CENTER>
<HR NOSHADE SIZE=2 WIDTH=500 ALIGN=CENTER>
<IMG SRC="elenacomputer.gif" WIDTH=170 HEIGHT=175 BORDER=0
ALT="This is me!" ALIGN=LEFT VSPACE=10 HSPACE=25>
<FONT SIZE=2 COLOR="blue" FACE="arial, helvetica">
<P><B>Hi!</B> My name is Elena, and this is my <I>Little House on the
Web</I>.</P>
<P>I made it…</P>
<UL>
<LI>to tell everyone about me
<LI>to link up with my friends
<LI>to get extra credit from Mr. Abee
<LI>to have the coolest place in cyberspace
</UL>
</FONT>
<BR CLEAR>
```

(rest of the document stays the same)

Here is the revised Web page.

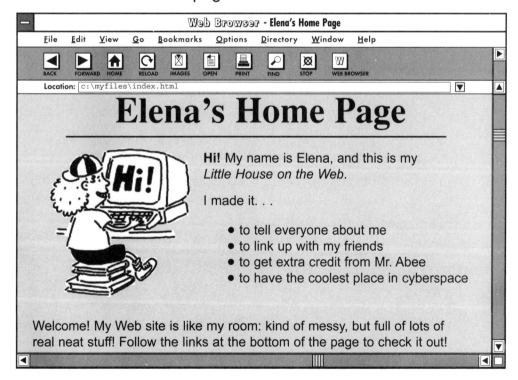

Notice that even though we got rid of the <BLOCKQUOTE> tags around the blue text, there is still some empty space between the blue text and the right side of the image. This is due to the HSPACE that we added. Notice also that now there is a little more room between the bottom of the image and the red text below it. This is due to the added VSPACE.

Linking to Other Pages on Your Web Site

HyperText links, or *hyperlinks*, are what make the World Wide Web interactive. The Web is made up of millions of different Web pages and Web sites connected by these hyperlinks. You probably already know that hyperlinks on a Web page usually appear as underlined, colored text. And when you position your mouse over a hyperlink, your cursor turns into a little pointing hand. Click on one of these hyperlinks and you are able to jump from one place on the Web to another.

Of course, if you are making only one Web page, you don't need to have hyperlinks on your page if you don't want to. But if you are making a Web site with several pages, you need to link your pages together with hyperlinks. Also, you may decide that you want to link your Web page to a friend's Web page. You can easily do this by building a hyperlink to your friend's page, and having your friend build a hyperlink from his or her page to yours. In the next few sections of this book, we'll show you how to build all kinds of hyperlinks into your Web page.

To make any kind of hyperlink, you need to add an anchor tag (<A>) to your HTML document. Anchor tags might look pretty complicated. But they all follow the same basic pattern. Here is the pattern—not an actual anchor tag, but a pattern for one.

<A HREF="destination">hyperlink text</A>

The opening tag in the pattern is <A HREF="destination">. This is simply the anchor tag (<A>) combined with the HREF attribute (for "hyperlink reference"). Together, they signal the beginning of a hyperlink. The "destination" is the place on the Web where you will end up if you click on this hyperlink on the Web page. The destination could be a different place on the same Web page, a different Web page on the same site, or a different Web site altogether.

Let us give you an example of an actual opening anchor tag. Suppose Elena wants to put a hyperlink on her home page that will take visitors to the family page on her Web site. We'll call her family page **elenafamily .html**. We could write the opening anchor tag for that hyperlink like this.

```
<A HREF="elenafamily.html">
```

Notice that the file name of the destination appears in quotation marks. Also notice that only the file name is given—no folders or directories are included. So the Web browser will look for the file called **elenafamily.html** in the same directory as **index.html**. This link is called a *relative link*, because it gives its destination relative to the location of the **index.html**.

After this opening tag, we have to add the hyperlink text. The hyperlink text is what will appear as the colored, underlined text on the Web page itself. It is the actual text that you would click on to activate the hyperlink.

Suppose Elena wants the hyperlink text to appear as "My Family Page". This is how we would write the entire anchor tag from beginning to end.

```
<A HREF="elenafamily.html">My Family Page</A>
```

> **Note:** Every anchor tag must end with the </A> end tag.

Let's go ahead and build two hyperlinks on Elena's home page: one to her family page (**elenafamily.html**) and one to her hobby page (**elenahobbies.html**).

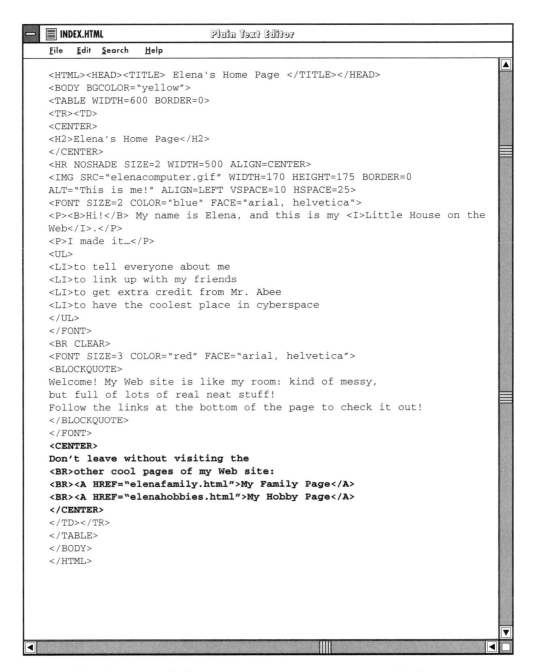

```
<HTML><HEAD><TITLE> Elena's Home Page </TITLE></HEAD>
<BODY BGCOLOR="yellow">
<TABLE WIDTH=600 BORDER=0>
<TR><TD>
<CENTER>
<H2>Elena's Home Page</H2>
</CENTER>
<HR NOSHADE SIZE=2 WIDTH=500 ALIGN=CENTER>
<IMG SRC="elenacomputer.gif" WIDTH=170 HEIGHT=175 BORDER=0
ALT="This is me!" ALIGN=LEFT VSPACE=10 HSPACE=25>
<FONT SIZE=2 COLOR="blue" FACE="arial, helvetica">
<P><B>Hi!</B> My name is Elena, and this is my <I>Little House on the
Web</I>.</P>
<P>I made it…</P>
<UL>
<LI>to tell everyone about me
<LI>to link up with my friends
<LI>to get extra credit from Mr. Abee
<LI>to have the coolest place in cyberspace
</UL>
</FONT>
<BR CLEAR>
<FONT SIZE=3 COLOR="red" FACE="arial, helvetica">
<BLOCKQUOTE>
Welcome! My Web site is like my room: kind of messy,
but full of lots of real neat stuff!
Follow the links at the bottom of the page to check it out!
</BLOCKQUOTE>
</FONT>
<CENTER>
Don't leave without visiting the
<BR>other cool pages of my Web site:
<BR><A HREF="elenafamily.html">My Family Page</A>
<BR><A HREF="elenahobbies.html">My Hobby Page</A>
</CENTER>
</TD></TR>
</TABLE>
</BODY>
</HTML>
```

Toward the bottom of Elena's HTML document, we added some new centered text, along with two anchor tags. The line break tags (<BR>) that we included will neatly format the new text and the hyperlinks on Elena's Web page. Take a look….

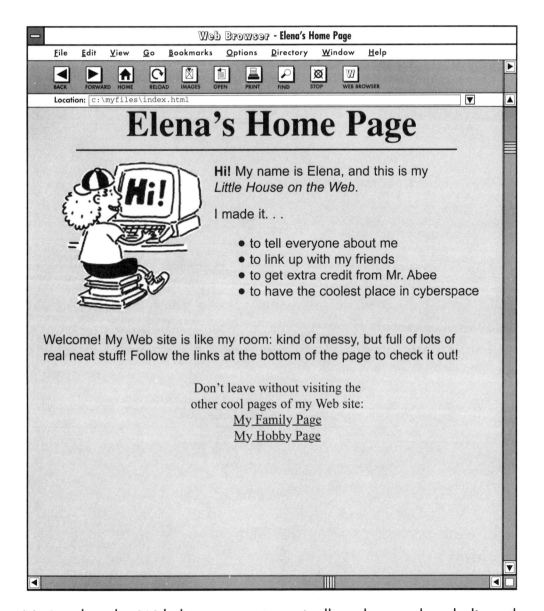

File   Edit   View   Go   Bookmarks   Options   Directory   Window   Help

BACK   FORWARD   HOME   RELOAD   IMAGES   OPEN   PRINT   FIND   STOP   WEB BROWSER

Location: `c:\myfiles\index.html`

Elena's Home Page

Hi! My name is Elena, and this is my *Little House on the Web.*

I made it. . .

- to tell everyone about me
- to link up with my friends
- to get extra credit from Mr. Abee
- to have the coolest place in cyberspace

Welcome! My Web site is like my room: kind of messy, but full of lots of real neat stuff! Follow the links at the bottom of the page to check it out!

Don't leave without visiting the
other cool pages of my Web site:
My Family Page
My Hobby Page

Notice that the Web browser automatically colors and underlines the hyperlink text so that it stands out on the Web page.

Of course, we can't really test these new hyperlinks without a family page and a hobby page to link to. So let's create a couple of very simple pages so that we can see if these hyperlinks really work.

Let's make the family page first. Open a new file on your text editor and make a new HTML document that looks like this.

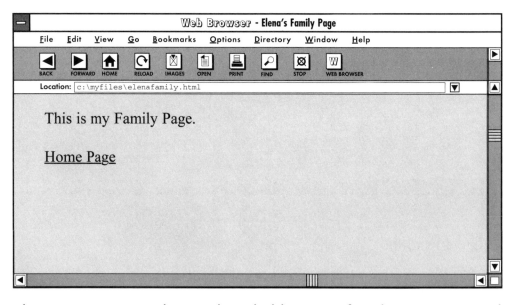

```
<HTML>
<HEAD>
<TITLE> Elena's Family Page </TITLE>
</HEAD>
<BODY>
<BR>
This is my Family Page.
<BR><BR>
<A HREF="index.html">Home Page</A>
</BODY>
</HTML>
```

Save your file as **elenafamily.html** in the same directory as your **index.html** document. Then switch to your Web browser and open **elenafamily.html**. You should see a very simple Web page that looks like this.

That was easy. Now let's make a hobby page for Elena. Open another new file in your text editor and make a new HTML document that looks like this.

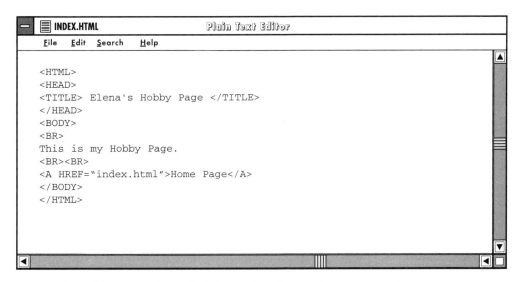

```
<HTML>
<HEAD>
<TITLE> Elena's Hobby Page </TITLE>
</HEAD>
<BODY>
<BR>
This is my Hobby Page.
<BR><BR>
<A HREF="index.html">Home Page</A>
</BODY>
</HTML>
```

Save this file as **elenahobbies.html** in the same directory as your **index.html** and **elenafamily.html** files. Then open **elenahobbies.html** in your Web browser, and you should see another simple Web page that looks like this.

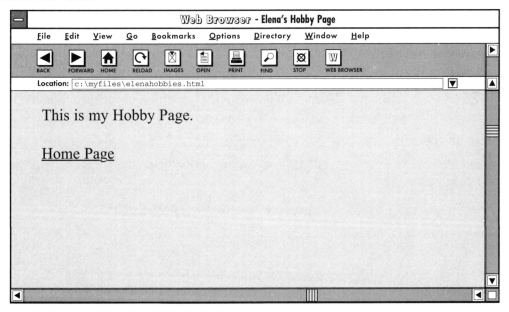

Now for the fun part.

Go back to the latest version of Elena's Home Page in your Web browser and go to the hyperlinks at the bottom. Click on the one that says "My Family Page." Magic! You're looking at the family page. Cool, huh?

Now, since we built a hyperlink back to the home page, you can click on it to return to Elena's Home Page. Remember, just because you build a link from your home page to another page on your site doesn't mean that there will <u>automatically</u> be a link back. Don't forget when you are building the other pages of your site to build hyperlinks back to **index.html**.

Linking to Other Web Sites

We said before that hyperlinks aren't just for connecting Web pages on the same Web site. You can also build links to connect your Web page to other Web sites on the Internet.

You build hyperlinks to other Web sites in the same way as you build links between pages on your own Web site. You use an anchor tag. But instead of a destination that is the name of a file on your computer (like **elenafamily.html**), you must insert the exact address of the other Web site. This kind of link is called an *absolute link*, because it gives its destination as a specific location on the World Wide Web.

Did you know that we have a Web site? We do! It's our *Internet for Kids* Web site, and it actually exists on the Internet. Just like every other Web site out there, our site has a *Uniform Resource Locator (URL)*, or a Web address. Our site's URL is **http://www.internet4kids.com**. (You are welcome to visit us anytime!)

If you wanted to build a hyperlink to our *Internet for Kids* Web site, you would need this anchor tag.

<A HREF="http://www.internet4kids.com">Internet For Kids</A>

This anchor tag would make a hyperlink on your Web page that reads "Internet for Kids." And if you clicked on that hyperlink, you would instantly jump to our Web site.

Let's add a link like that to Elena's page.

```
┌─────────────────────────────────────────────────────────────────┐
│ ─  📄 INDEX.HTML            Plain Text Editor                      │
├─────────────────────────────────────────────────────────────────┤
│    File   Edit   Search   Help                                    │
├─────────────────────────────────────────────────────────────────┤
                                                                  ▲
   <HTML><HEAD><TITLE> Elena's Home Page </TITLE></HEAD>
   <BODY BGCOLOR="yellow">
   <TABLE WIDTH=600 BORDER=0>
   <TR><TD>
   <CENTER>
   <H2>Elena's Home Page</H2>
   </CENTER>
   <HR NOSHADE SIZE=2 WIDTH=500 ALIGN=CENTER>
   <IMG SRC="elenacomputer.gif" WIDTH=170 HEIGHT=175 BORDER=0
   ALT="This is me!" ALIGN=LEFT VSPACE=10 HSPACE=25>
   <FONT SIZE=2 COLOR="blue" FACE="arial, helvetica">
   <P><B>Hi!</B> My name is Elena, and this is my <I>Little House on the
   Web</I>.</P>
   <P>I made it…</P>
   <UL>
   <LI>to tell everyone about me
   <LI>to link up with my friends
   <LI>to get extra credit from Mr. Abee
   <LI>to have the coolest place in cyberspace
   </UL>
   </FONT>
   <BR CLEAR>
   <FONT SIZE=3 COLOR="red" FACE="arial, helvetica">
   <BLOCKQUOTE>
   Welcome! My Web site is like my room: kind of messy,
   but full of lots of real neat stuff!
   Follow the links at the bottom of the page to check it out!
   </BLOCKQUOTE>
   </FONT>
   <CENTER>
   Don't leave without visiting the
   <BR>other cool pages of my Web site:
   <BR><A HREF="elenafamily.html">My Family Page</A>
   <BR><A HREF="elenahobbies.html">My Hobby Page</A>
   </CENTER>
   <BR><BR>
   <FONT SIZE=2>
   <CENTER>
   I couldn't have built this Web site without help from my
   friends at:
   <A HREF="http://www.internet4kids.com">
   www.internet4kids.com</A>.
   </CENTER>
   </FONT>
   </TD></TR>
   </TABLE>
   </BODY>
   </HTML>
                                                                  ▼
└─────────────────────────────────────────────────────────────────┘
```

As you can see, we added the new anchor tag at the bottom of the HTML document. So the new hyperlink that it makes on the Web page will appear on the bottom of the page. We put the anchor tag inside some new text, and used the <CENTER> tag and the <FONT SIZE=2> tag to make the text centered and smaller than usual. (Notice that we did <u>not</u> specify a typeface or color for the new text. This means that the Web browser will display the text in black, and in its standard or default font.)

All of this new code makes for a nice little footnote to Elena's page, as you can see here.

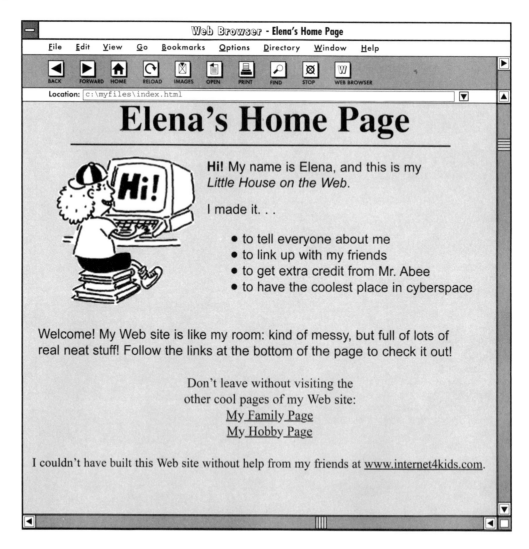

Linking to Other Places on the Same Web Page

You can also build hyperlinks that will take you from one place on a Web page to another place on the same page. Why would you want to build a link like this? Well, let's say that your home page is very long, and the hyperlinks to your other pages are way down at the bottom of the home page. You can put a hyperlink near the top of your page that will immediately take visitors down to the bottom.

> **Tip:** If you build a hyperlink from the top to the bottom of a long page, don't forget to build a reverse link that will take viewers back to the top of your page.

Just like the other types of hyperlinks we have talked about, you build links within a page by using an anchor tag. But unlike the other hyperlinks, you need to add two separate anchor tags to make this kind of link. One of these anchor tags follows the same basic pattern we have already learned. It tells the Web browser the destination of the hyperlink and gives the hyperlink text that will appear on the Web page.

But for links within a page, you need an additional anchor tag that works a little differently. It marks the spot on the page—the *target*—that the hyperlink will jump to. It's like a signpost to the Web browser that says "Jump Here!" whenever that hyperlink is clicked.

First, let's take a look at the pattern for building a target.

```
<A NAME="target name">target text</A>
```

In this pattern, the opening tag is simply the anchor tag <A> combined with the NAME attribute. We use the NAME attribute to give our target a name, and we put it in quotation marks. You can give a target any name you like.

Between the opening tag in the pattern (<A NAME="target name">) and the end tag (</A>) comes the "target text." This is the text that will actually appear on your Web page wherever you place the target.

Now let's look at the pattern for building the hyperlink that jumps to the target. You'll notice that it is very similar to the pattern we talked about in the earlier sections on hyperlinks.

<A HREF="#target name">hyperlink text</A>

As we learned earlier, the anchor tag <A> combined with the HREF attribute signals the beginning of a hyperlink. As the destination for this hyperlink, you put the name of the target that it will jump to, preceded by a number sign (#). Notice that the target name and the number sign are in quotation marks. Then, between this opening tag and the end tag </A>, comes the "hyperlink text." This will appear on your Web page as the colored, underlined text of the hyperlink.

Don't worry if you are still a little bit confused about building hyperlinks within a page. Now we are going to put these patterns into practice by adding one of these hyperlinks to Elena's page, and things should become much clearer.

On Elena's page, let's make a hyperlink out of the word "links" (which appears in the red block of text). And let's make it so that this hyperlink jumps down to the "My Family Page" and "My Hobby Page" links at the bottom of her page. To do this, we can build around the text that already exists on Elena's page. Here is what we add.

```
┌──────────────────────────────────────────────────────────────────────┐
│ ▤ INDEX.HTML              Plain Text Editor                          │
├──────────────────────────────────────────────────────────────────────┤
│  File   Edit   Search   Help                                          │
├──────────────────────────────────────────────────────────────────────┤
```

<HTML><HEAD><TITLE> Elena's Home Page </TITLE></HEAD>
<BODY BGCOLOR="yellow">
<TABLE WIDTH=600 BORDER=0>
<TR><TD>
<CENTER>
<H2>Elena's Home Page</H2>
</CENTER>
<HR NOSHADE SIZE=2 WIDTH=500 ALIGN=CENTER>
<IMG SRC="elenacomputer.gif" WIDTH=170 HEIGHT=175 BORDER=0
ALT="This is me!" ALIGN=LEFT VSPACE=10 HSPACE=25>
<FONT SIZE=2 COLOR="blue" FACE="arial, helvetica">
<P><B>Hi!</B> My name is Elena, and this is my <I>Little House on the
Web</I>.</P>
<P>I made it…</P>
<UL>
<LI>to tell everyone about me
<LI>to link up with my friends
<LI>to get extra credit from Mr. Abee
<LI>to have the coolest place in cyberspace
</UL>
</FONT>
<BR CLEAR>
<FONT SIZE=3 COLOR="red" FACE="arial, helvetica">
<BLOCKQUOTE>
Welcome! My Web site is like my room: kind of messy,
but full of lots of real neat stuff!
Follow the **<A HREF="#menu">**links**</A>** at the bottom of the
page to check it out!
</BLOCKQUOTE>
</FONT>
**

**
**

**
<CENTER>
<A NAME="menu">Don't leave without visiting the**</A>**

other cool pages of my Web site:

<A HREF="elenafamily.html">My Family Page</A>

<A HREF="elenahobbies.html">My Hobby Page</A>
</CENTER>

<FONT SIZE=2>
<CENTER>
I couldn't have built this Web site without help from my
friends at:
<A HREF="http://www.internet4kids.com">
www.internet4kids.com</A>.
</CENTER>
</FONT>
</TD></TR>
</TABLE>
</BODY>
</HTML>

By adding these new pieces of HTML code, we have done three things.

1. With the <A NAME="menu"> tag, we have placed the target at the line of text that reads: "Don't leave without visiting the…" And we have given the target a name: "menu." We closed the anchor tag with the end tag </A>.
2. We have identified "links" as the hyperlink text by placing the <A HREF="#menu"> tag before it, and the </A> tag after it. It will appear on the Web page as the colored, underlined text of the link.
3. We have added twenty new <BR> tags between the red block of text and the "Don't leave…" text. We will take these line breaks out later. We have put them in for now so that the two blocks of text don't appear on the same screen together. Otherwise you wouldn't really need a hyperlink to skip down to the bottom of the page.

Now save the revised HTML document and check out the new Web page. We won't show you the updated Web page here because the only visible changes are 1) the word "links" has transformed into the colored, underlined text of a hyperlink; and 2) there is a bunch of space following the red block of text. On the new page, test out your newest hyperlink by clicking on the word "links" and seeing what happens. You want to be at the upper part of the page so that when you click, the browser window will move down to the bottom of the Web page.

Linking to Get E-mail

Another thing you might want to do on your Web site is encourage people to send you e-mail to tell you how they like it. You can make this very convenient for people by including a special kind of hyperlink on your Web page. It is called a *mail-to link*.

When a visitor to your Web page clicks on a mail-to hyperlink, his or her e-mail program automatically opens up, and a new blank mail message—already addressed and ready to go—appears on the screen! Your visitors can type their messages right then and there. What could be simpler?

Just like every other hyperlink, you build a mail-to link with (you guessed it!) an anchor tag. You'll see that the anchor tag pattern for this kind of link is very similar to the other hyperlink patterns.

Take a look at an example. Let's say that Elena wants to put a mail-to link on her home page, so that people can send her mail. And let's say that her e-mail address is **elena@internet4kids.com**. Here is the opening anchor tag that she would need.

<A HREF="mailto:elena@internet4kids.com">

> **Note:** This e-mail address for Elena is a real one, and you can use it to send her an e-note at our *Internet for Kids* Web site.

Then, between this opening tag and the end tag </A>, Elena must put the hyperlink text that she wants to appear on her Web page. In the case of mail-to links, it's a good idea to use the actual e-mail address as the hyperlink text. Why? First of all, visitors to your Web site must have their browsers set up to send e-mail in order for them to use your mail-to link. If their browser is not set up properly, they'll need to take down your address and open up their e-mail program to send you a message. Also, what if a visitor to your site printed out your Web page, and then looked at it later and wanted to send you a message? If you put something like "To e-mail me, click here" as your hyperlink text, that visitor would have no idea what your e-mail address is.

A mail-to link doesn't have to link to <u>your</u> e-mail address. Maybe your friend is a stamp collector, and he asked you to put a note on your Web page asking other stamp enthusiasts to e-mail him. You could simply substitute his e-mail address as the destination of the mail-to link.

Elena wants to add a mail-to link to her Web page. She thinks it would be really cool to get messages from people all over the world—especially if they were messages on her favorite subjects: books and movies!

"I know," says Elena. "I could ask people to e-mail me and tell me about their favorite book or movie!"

Elena gets ready to add her mail-to link to her HTML document. Then she remembers another picture that she wanted to add to her Web page. It's a little drawing of some books all in a row. Perfect! She can put this image on her Web page—right next to a little block of text that contains her mail-to link.

"This time I'm going to align my image against the right side of my Web page," she says. "And I'll wrap my text around the left side."

Here's how we can add the new image, new text, and the mail-to link to Elena's page. The first half of the HTML document stays the same. We will just show you the second half—the part that contains the changes.

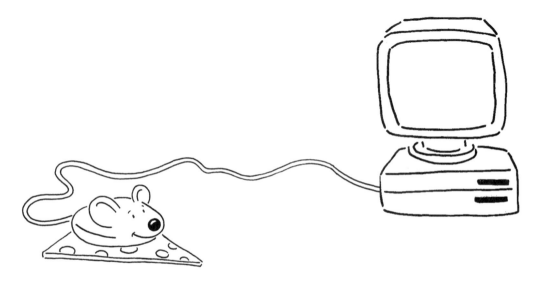

File　Edit　Search　Help

(document stays the same up to this point)

```
<BLOCKQUOTE>
Welcome! My Web site is like my room: kind of messy,
but full of lots of real neat stuff!
Follow the <A HREF="#menu">links</A> at the bottom of the
page to check it out!
</BLOCKQUOTE>
</FONT>
<BR><BR><BR>
<IMG SRC="elenabooks.gif" WIDTH=250 HEIGHT=75 BORDER=2
ALT="Books!" ALIGN=RIGHT VSPACE=10 HSPACE=10>
<FONT SIZE=2 COLOR="maroon" FACE="arial">
<BLOCKQUOTE>
<P>I really love to read books and watch movies
when I'm not busy surfing the Web. Tell me about
your favorite book or movie, or anything else, by
e-mailing me at <A HREF="mailto:elena@internet4kids.com">
elena@internet4kids.com</A>.
</BLOCKQUOTE>
<BR CLEAR>
</FONT>
<BR><BR>
<CENTER>
<A NAME="menu">Don't leave without visiting the</A>
<BR>other cool pages of my Web site:
<BR><A HREF="elenafamily.html">My Family Page</A>
<BR><A HREF="elenahobbies.html">My Hobby Page</A>
</CENTER>
<BR><BR>
<FONT SIZE=2>
<CENTER>
I couldn't have built this Web site without help from my
friends at:
<A HREF="http://www.internet4kids.com">
www.internet4kids.com</A>.
</CENTER>
</FONT>
</TD></TR>
</TABLE>
</BODY>
</HTML>
```

Whew! That's a lot of new code. (Notice that we also deleted most of those <BR> tags that we had in the last version of our HTML document.) Since you're getting to be such an expert on HTML, you can probably figure out what each piece of the new code will do. But let's take a closer look at it anyway.

First, we put in a new <IMG> tag for the new picture called **elenabooks.gif**.

We defined the WIDTH and the HEIGHT. We added a BORDER around the image (so that you could see where it would appear on the Web page), and we gave some ALT text ("Books!"). We aligned the image against the right side of the Web page, and put 10 pixels of VSPACE and HSPACE around it.

Next, we added a new <FONT> tag to define the SIZE, COLOR, and FACE of the text that follows (which is the text that will wrap around the left side of the new image). Then we typed in the actual text and the anchor tag for the mail-to link inside a <BLOCKQUOTE> tag. Finally, we added the <BR CLEAR> tag to mark the end of the text that should wrap around the new image.

The new Web page looks pretty cool, don't you think? (Remember that the picture of the books will not appear on your screen.)

Link Colors

We can't end our section on hyperlinks without telling you how to make them different colors! As we have seen, the Web browser will automatically display hyperlinks on your page in a different color than the surrounding text. But you can specify exactly what color you want them to be. Do you remember that to specify a background color for your Web page, you add the BGCOLOR attribute inside the <BODY> tag of your HTML document? Well, you do basically the same thing to choose a color for your hyperlinks—except that you use the LINK attribute inside the<BODY> tag.

Here is a <BODY> tag with a LINK attribute and a BGCOLOR attribute inside it.

```
<BODY BGCOLOR="yellow" LINK="blue">
```

This tag tells the Web browser to put a yellow background on the Web page, and to display all of the hyperlinks on the page in blue text.

On some Web pages—especially a page that has a lot of hyperlinks on it—it is helpful to pick a different color for visited links (or VLINKs). This helps visitors keep track of the places on your site where they have already been. Let's say you are visiting Elena's Web site. You jump from the home page to the family page. Then you jump back. When you return to the home page—if Elena used the VLINK attribute in her HTML document—the hyperlink "My Family Page" would be displayed in a different color. This change in color lets you know that you have already visited the family page.

You use the same color words and hex codes to specify link colors as you did to specify text and background colors. For the complete list, refer back to page 32.

Let's add LINK and VLINK attributes to Elena's HTML document. For now, we'll choose some really bright, vivid colors. Since we are only adding a little bit of new code, we will only show the first few lines of the revised document—the part that contains the change.

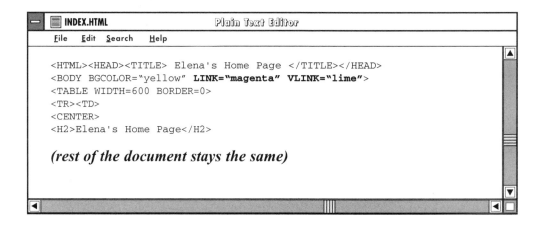

```
INDEX.HTML                    Plain Text Editor
 File   Edit   Search   Help

<HTML><HEAD><TITLE> Elena's Home Page </TITLE></HEAD>
<BODY BGCOLOR="yellow" LINK="magenta" VLINK="lime">
<TABLE WIDTH=600 BORDER=0>
<TR><TD>
<CENTER>
<H2>Elena's Home Page</H2>

(rest of the document stays the same)
```

Be sure to save the changes before switching to your Web browser to see the updated Web page. This is another place in our black-and-white book where we can't show you the color changes on the Web page. But you should be able to view the changes on your own computer screen.

> **Note:** Until you have posted your Web site on the Internet, you can only test the VLINK color of the relative links on your site; that is, those links that jump to other places within your Web site.

Compare the Web page you now see on your screen with Elena's Home Page on the back cover of this book. Looks pretty similar, right? But you probably notice one major difference. The heading on your page is in a regular typeface and all in one color (black). On the back cover, Elena's page has a multi-colored heading and looks like it is hand-written. How would you do something like that?

Well, Elena decided to use an image as the heading for her home page. She used her paint program to create a multicolored heading. Then, just like the other two images on her home page, she made sure the image file was in the appropriate format (either GIF or JPEG). Finally, she added a new <IMG> tag to her HTML document that would center this new heading image at the top of her Web page. Not complicated at all, really! Of course, it's important to remember that, if visitors to Elena's Web site have their image displays turned off, they won't be able to see Elena's cool heading. So, before you use an image for a heading on your page, give some thought to whether or not the page will look okay without it.

Presto! A Finished Web Page

Congratulations! You have just built a really nice-looking and fully operational Web page, and you should be very proud of yourself. Take a minute to admire your handiwork. What do you think? Are there certain things that you would like to change? Do you have ideas for making the page even better? Or do you want to start all over with a blank HTML document and build a page that is all your own? You can!

Don't feel bound by Elena's Home Page. This is only one example of what you can do with the things you have learned. You can use this practice Web page as a training ground. Experiment with different things and get even more comfortable with HTML. Then, when you're ready, start building your own page. If you start writing new code and don't get things right the first time, don't worry! The worst thing that can happen is that your Web page won't look exactly the way you meant it to. (And it might look even better than what you had in mind.) No matter what, you can always go back to your HTML document and fiddle some more until you are happy with the results.

You now have the tools to make some pretty fantastic Web pages. But at the same time, we have only scratched the surface of HTML and what it can do. Later on in the book, we'll tell you where you can go to learn even more about designing and building Web pages. But in this next section, we'll focus on how to get your finished Web pages up and running on the Internet.

𝟹
LAUNCHING YOUR WEB SITE

So your Web site is finally built. It looks really cool on the Web browser on your computer. Now it's time to post your site on the World Wide Web so everyone will be able to enjoy it.

In order to make your Web pages accessible to everyone on the Internet, you need to take all of the HTML files and graphics files for your Web pages and store them on a *Web server*. A Web server is a computer that is connected to the Internet twenty-four hours a day. Once your files are stored on a Web server, people all over the world will be able to visit your Web page on the Internet.

You could set up your own Web server. But that would be very expensive. Most people posting Web pages get space for their files on Web servers that are owned and maintained by companies. For example, many of the most popular *Internet service providers* (or ISPs) will reserve a certain amount of space on their Web servers for their customers' Web pages.

So, here is what you need to post your Web pages.

1. You need to find space on a Web server where you can store the files for your Web pages. If you already have Internet access from home, call your ISP (or have an adult call for you) and ask if they can provide space for your site. There are also free Web host sites, like GeoCities (**http://www.geocities.com**), which will host your Web site for free.
2. You'll need a *File Transfer Protocol* (FTP) program (like WS_FTP for Windows, or FETCH for Macs) that will transfer your HTML and image files to the Web server.

Once you have space on a Web server and an FTP program, you are ready to upload your files to your Web host site. Exactly how you do this will depend upon the FTP program you use, and on your Web host.

Always check with your Web host before you start transferring any files. Most Web hosts will be able to give you a simple step-by-step process for uploading files. They will also give you information on exactly where your space on the Web server is; in other words, which directory on the Web server you should store your files in. Your Web host might also have certain rules about how your files should be named and organized. And finally, you will need to get a user name or ID, and a password from your Web host in order to connect to the Web server and load your files. So, once again, it is very important that you get all of the information you need from your Web host before you transfer any files.

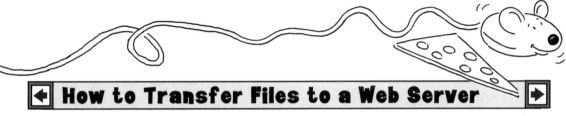

How to Transfer Files to a Web Server

As we said, the steps for uploading files will vary depending upon the FTP program you use and your Web server. But just to give you an idea, here is how we would load our *Internet for Kids* pages onto the Rent-A-Web ISP, using a Windows FTP program called WS_FTP. (Just remember: Even if you have this exact FTP program and are signed up with this Web host, contact your Web host for instructions on transferring your files. The process may have changed since the publication of this book.)

1. Log on to the Internet.
2. Open your FTP program.
3. You will see a window titled "Session Profile." Click NEW to create a new profile, and type in a Profile Name (like "My Web Site").
4. Type in the name of your Web host.
5. Make sure your Host Type is set to "Automatic Detect" so the program uses the right method to send text or binary files.

6. Type in your Login name or User ID.

7. Type in your secret password. Because it's secret, you'll see ***** instead of the actual password, in case anyone is looking over your shoulder.

8. Type in the name of your local directory (the directory on your computer) where you have saved your HTML and graphic files. Remember to have all of these files saved in the same directory on your computer.

9. Make your connection to the Web host site by clicking the "Connect" button.

10. You should see two windows. The one on the left is the directory on your computer where your files are saved. The one on the right is the directory on the Web server. (In most cases, this directory will be called **public.html**.)

11. One at a time, transfer your files to the Web server directory. The method you use will vary for different FTP programs, but usually you will highlight the file you want to send, and then send the file (usually using an arrow or a SEND button). When a file has been sent, it will appear in the Web server directory window.

12. Do this for all the files you want to send. Make sure that you send HTML files in ASCII (plain text) format and graphic files in binary format.

13. Once you've transferred all the files, close your connection and exit the program.

> **Note:** If you have a file—for example, an image file—that appears on more than one Web page, you only have to upload that file to the Web server once.

That's it! It's a good idea now to open your Web browser and go to your Web site. (You will have to find out from your Web host what the

URL, or Web address, of your Web site is.) Make sure that your pages look the way you want them to look. Test all of the hyperlinks on your site, and make sure that all of your images are there. If they aren't, you may have forgotten to send one of the files.

If, when you check your pages on the Internet, things don't look quite right or you find a mistake that you never noticed, don't worry. Later on in the book, we'll talk about how to make changes to your Web site once it is already posted.

Tip: A word about file names: Some Web servers distinguish between UPPER-CASE letters and lowercase letters. So be careful when saving your files. A picture might not be found because you uploaded it to the Web server as **Picture.gif** while it is named in your HTML file as **picture.gif**.

Promoting Your Web Site

You've got your Web site loaded onto your ISP. But how do you tell people about it so they can visit?

1. E-mail your friends and relatives. This is the direct approach. Send out an announcement about your Web site to all your family and friends who have e-mail. Keep it simple and to the point, like:

Hi! I've just put my own Web site online. Please visit me at:
http://www.internet4kids.com/elena

2. Send announcements of your new Web site to newsgroups that might be interested. It's a good idea to read those newsgroups you've selected for a few days before posting your announcement. That way, you can get a good sense of what the newsgroups are about and make sure that your announcement would be appropriate. Remember to keep your announcement short and to the point.

3. Make your page link to *Internet for Kids!* If you want to, you can add a hyperlink from your Web page to our own **www.internet4kids.com** Web page, just like Elena did. And, if you send us an e-mail note telling us that you did, we'll even build a link on our page back to yours. All the instructions are online at our Web site. Come check it out!

4. Register your Web page with popular search engines, like Yahoo, HotBot, AltaVista, and InfoSeek. All major search engines have places where you can register your site.

- Yahoo (**http://www.yahoo.com**) is one of the most popular directory sites on the Web.

- Yahooligans (**http://www.yahooligans.com**) is the junior edition of Yahoo. Like its big brother, it is a must for registering your Web site.

- Hotbot (**http://www.hotbot.com**) is one of the best search engines around.

- AltaVista (**http://www.altavista.digital.com**) is perhaps the most complete search engine on the Web.

- Infoseek (**http://www.infoseek.com**) and Lycos (**http://www.lycos.com**) are two more very popular search engines.

There are a lot of other directories and search engines out there. You can spend days just registering your Web site with all of them, but these key sites will get you off to a good start.

With her Web site now on the World Wide Web, Elena tells everyone she knows. The computer instructor at Elena's school gives her a great piece of advice for promoting her site: "Make a good META tag," he tells her.

If you decide to register your Web page with a search engine, it's a good idea to put a <META> tag into your **index.html** document. A <META> tag identifies the topics that your Web page covers. Search engines will read your <META> tag when they search the Web for pages on particular topics.

For example, let's say that there is someone who enjoys books just as much as Elena does. He uses a search engine one day to search for Web sites on books. If Elena has registered her Web site with that search engine, and if she has used a <META> tag to signal that her Web site has something to do with books, then Elena's Home Page would turn up on the search engine's list of sites.

A <META> tag is a stand-alone tag. (It has no end tag.) You can put a <META> tag anywhere between the <HEAD> and </HEAD> tags in your HTML document.

Here is a <META> tag that Elena might include in her **index.html** header.

<META NAME="KEYWORDS" CONTENT="Elena, family, fun, hobby, books, movies">

To make your own <META> tag, follow the same pattern and simply substitute your own keywords following the CONTENT attribute. Make sure that you separate the words with commas, and put them all inside quotation marks. You can list as many words as you like. Think about the key words that best describe your site.

Okay, we're only going to say it one more time. Building a Web site is like building a house. And as with a house, you'll want to do some remodeling from time to time. We found that many of the Web sites we looked at while writing the first edition of *Internet for Kids!* had been remodeled by the time we looked at them for the revised edition of the book. The nice thing about publishing on the Web is that if you make a mistake, you can correct it almost instantly.

There are three steps to making changes to your Web site.

1. In your text editor, re-open the HTML document you want to change.

2. Make the changes and save the file.

3. Connect to the Internet and upload your changed files to your Web server.

If you are adding new pages to your Web site, don't forget to change the menus on your other pages and build more hyperlinks so that your viewers can connect to the new page. And don't forget to tell your viewers when you last updated your page. One way to do this is to put a comment at the bottom of your pages to note when you last updated that page. You can do it like this:

1. Just before the closing </HTML> tag, type in **<H5>**.

2. Now type in something like **This page was last updated on 12.31.98**.

3. Finally, type in **</H5>**.

Of course, you'll want to change 12.31.98 to the correct date. The <H5> tag will yield small text and is a good choice for this kind of footnote.

Building a Web site, or at least writing the HTML code, isn't that hard. What can be more difficult is designing a nice, simple page that will attract visitors. So spend a lot of time imagining and planning your pages before you actually start to build them. If this is your first Web site, consider making it a family affair, or doing it as project in your classroom or with your friends.

There are a lot of places online to get help. Use a search engine to search the Web for more information on HTML. One of our favorite reference Web sites is the "Web building" section of CNET. You can find it at **http://www.cnet.com**.

And check out our page at **http://www.internet4kids.com**. We have a special section there on building a Web site. We'll be listing new tips and tricks, and we'll have links to Web design tutorials and suggestions of places to go to download software and image files.

Another excellent way to learn more HTML tags is to look at the HTML files of other Web pages. If you are browsing the Web and find a Web page that you really like, you can see the HTML document behind it by clicking on VIEW in the top bar of your Web browser window, and selecting DOCUMENT SOURCE. Instantly, you will see the entire HTML document for that Web page on your computer screen. Sometimes it's very interesting to see how other people put their pages together. Get ideas from other pages, but feel free to make your Web page completely different from any other you have seen.

Because in the end, your page is all your own. And even though there are millions of other Web pages already out in cyberspace, there's plenty of room for yours. Be creative, and have fun!

Glossary

Anchor - A tag used to build a hyperlink or a target in your HTML document.

Attribute - An additional part of a tag that provides an extra instruction to the Web browser.

Body - The "heart" of an HTML document; the part between the <BODY> and </BODY> tags where the text, pictures, and hyperlinks that will appear on the Web page are inserted.

File Transfer Protocol - A method of sending files from one computer to another over the Internet. To post a page on the World Wide Web, an FTP program is required to transfer HTML and image files to a Web server.

GIF file - One of the two basic graphic files used on the Web; GIF files have the **.gif** extension.

Header - The part of an HTML document—between the <HEAD> and </HEAD> tags—where you can title the Web page and add <META> tags.

Home page - The opening page of a Web site.

Hyperlink - A link connecting one part of the World Wide Web to another part; usually indicated on a Web page by colored text or a border around an image.

Hypertext - Colored or formatted text on a Web page that signals a hyper-link.

HyperText Markup Language (HTML) - The basic computer language in which Web pages are written.

Internet service provider (ISP) - A company that provides access to the Internet.

JPEG file - One of the two basic graphic files used on the Web; JPEG files have the **.jpg** extension and are generally used for storing photographs.

Search engine - A system dedicated to the search and retrieval of information on the Internet.

Tag - Letters or words placed between angle brackets that act as formatting commands in an HTML document.

Text Editor - Any program that will let you create and edit text files.

Uniform Resource Locator (URL) - The standard method of expressing the location, or "address," of a Web page on the World Wide Web.

Web browser - A program that reads HTML files and displays them as Web pages.

Web page - An HTML document as seen through a Web browser.

Web server - A computer that stores Web pages and is connected to the Internet twenty-four hours a day.

Web site - A collection of Web pages—usually linked together with hyperlinks—stored together on a Web server.

Index

absolute links, 66
AltaVista, 84
alternative text, 52
angle brackets, 16
ASCII files, 15, 19
attributes, 29, 88

blockquotes, 36-37
body, 17, 88
boldfaced text, 26, 28
borders, 45, 46, 52

clip-art packages, 9, 49
CNET, 87
colors:
  background, 46-47, 77
  of hyperlinks, 63, 77-78
  of text, 31-34
copyright, 9

Dreamweaver, 4

e-mail, 72-74, 83
  hyperlinks and, 72-76

FETCH, 80
files, uploading of, 80-83
File Transfer Protocol (FTP) program,
80-82, 88
fonts, 29-34
FrontPage, 4

GeoCities, 80
GIF files, 48, 49, 78, 88

header, 17, 88

headings, 20-22, 34-35
home pages, 11-12, 88
horizontal rules, 37-40
Hotbot, 84
HTML, 1, 4-7, 79, 87, 88
  files in, 18, 80
  programs for writing in, 6
  using, 14-79
  Web browsers and, 6
hyperlinks, 13, 60-78, 83, 86, 88
  to get e-mail, 72-76
  between pages in Web site, 60-66
  within same Web page, 69-72
  between Web sites, 66-68
HyperText Markup Language, see HTML

images, on Web sites, 48-59, 78-79, 80
Infoseek, 84
Internet, 1, 6, 17, 54, 80
  searching of, 2-3, 5, 9, 84-85, 87,
  89
  speed of access to, 12, 52, 54
Internet for Kids! (Pedersen and Moss),
86, 90
Internet for Kids Web site, 66-68, 84,
87, 90
Internet service providers (ISPs), 80-81,
88
italic text, 26, 28

JPEG files, 48, 49, 78, 88

line breaks, 23-26
lists, 40-42
Lycos, 84

Macintosh, 6, 50, 80
mail-to links, 72-76
META tags, 85
Microsoft Internet Explorer, 6
Microsoft Word, 6

Netscape Navigator, 6
Notepad, 6

PageMill, 4
paint programs, 50, 78
Paint Shop Pro, 50
paragraphs, formatting of, 23-26, 35-37

relative links, 61

scanning, of photos and drawings, 48, 49
search engines, 84-85, 87, 89
ShareDraw, 50
SimpleText, 6

tables, 42-46
tags, 16, 18, 89
  anchor, 60-62, 68, 69-70, 73, 76, 88
  blockquote, 36-37, 58, 60
  body, 17, 46, 77
  for boldface, 26, 28
  for centering headings, 34-35
  font, 29-34, 76
  header, 17
  heading, 21-22
  for horizontal rules, 37-40
  image, 49-52, 54-56, 58, 75-76
  for italics, 26, 28
  line break, 23-26
  list, 40-42
  META, 85
  paragraph, 24, 35-36

table, 43-45
  for text size, 31
  for underlining, 27
text, 7, 10-11, 54-57
  color of, 31-34
  font of, 29-31
  size of, 31
text editors, 4, 5-6, 14, 15, 17-18, 89
text wrapping, 54-57

underlined text, 27
Uniform Resource Locator (URL), 66, 83, 89
uploading files, 80-83

Web browsers, 4, 6, 14, 16, 17-18, 89
Web pages, 2, 12, 14, 89
Web servers, 80-83, 89
Web sites, 1, 2-3, 89
  building of, 7, 14-79, 87
  creating of, 1, 4-5
  imagining of, 7, 8-11
  launching of, 80-85
  maintaining of, 86
  planning of, 7, 11-13
  promoting of, 83-85
  types of, 1, 2-3
Windows, 6, 50, 80
Wordpad, 6
WordPerfect, 6
word processing programs, 5-6, 24
World Wide Web, 1, 7
  hyperlinks and, 60
  posting Web site to, 80-83
WS_FTP, 80

Yahoo, 84
Yahooligans, 2, 84

About the Authors

Together **Ted Pedersen** and **Francis Moss** have written the popular *Internet for Kids!* book. They have also collaborated on scripts for many animated television shows, including *X-Men*, *Pocket Dragons*, *Mummies Alive!*, *Teenage Mutant Ninja Turtles*, and *Exosquad*.

Ted Pedersen is the author of four *StarTrek: Deep Space Nine* novels for young readers, as well as *The Tale of the Virtual Nightmare* for the *Are You Afraid of the Dark?* book series and four *Cybersurfer* novels. Ted lives in Venice, California, with his wife, Phyllis, and several cats and computers. Ted is on the Web at **http://www.timetrek.com**.

Francis Moss has written and story edited for many television shows including *Care Bears*, *Teenage Mutant Ninja Turtles*, and *James Bond, Jr.* He is a contributing writer for *Using Windows 95, Special Edition*, reviews CD ROM games for online publications, and is a designer of Web sites. His next book, *The Rosenberg Trial*, is due out in 1999. He lives with his family in North Hollywood, California. Francis is on the Net at **fcmoss@internet4kids.com**.

Internet for Kids! is on the Web at **http://www.internet4kids.com**. You can go there to get more tips on creating Web sites. You can find Elena's finished Web site there, including all the images she used, plus a lot of other images you can download and use on your own Web site.

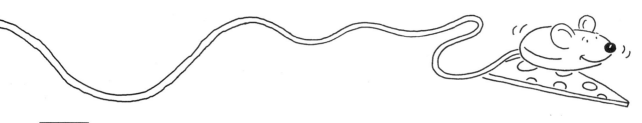